Slovenia

WORLD BIBLIOGRAPHICAL SERIES

General Editors:
Robert G. Neville (Executive Editor)
John J. Horton

Robert A. Myers   Hans H. Wellisch
Ian Wallace   Ralph Lee Woodward, Jr.

John J. Horton is Deputy Librarian of the University of Bradford and was formerly Chairman of its Academic Board of Studies in Social Sciences. He has maintained a longstanding interest in the discipline of area studies and its associated bibliographical problems, with special reference to European Studies. In particular he has published in the field of Icelandic and of Yugoslav studies, including the two relevant volumes in the World Bibliographical Series.

Robert A. Myers is Associate Professor of Anthropology in the Division of Social Sciences and Director of Study Abroad Programs at Alfred University, Alfred, New York. He has studied post-colonial island nations of the Caribbean and has spent two years in Nigeria on a Fulbright Lectureship. His interests include international public health, historical anthropology and developing societies. In addition to *Amerindians of the Lesser Antilles: a bibliography* (1981), *A Resource Guide to Dominica, 1493-1986* (1987) and numerous articles, he has compiled the World Bibliographical Series volumes on *Dominica* (1987), *Nigeria* (1989) and *Ghana* (1991).

Ian Wallace is Professor of German at the University of Bath. A graduate of Oxford in French and German, he also studied in Tübingen, Heidelberg and Lausanne before taking teaching posts at universities in the USA, Scotland and England. He specializes in contemporary German affairs, especially literature and culture, on which he has published numerous articles and books. In 1979 he founded the journal *GDR Monitor*, which he continues to edit under its new title *German Monitor*.

Hans H. Wellisch is Professor emeritus at the College of Library and Information Services, University of Maryland. He was President of the American Society of Indexers and was a member of the International Federation for Documentation. He is the author of numerous articles and several books on indexing and abstracting, and has published *The Conversion of Scripts and Indexing and Abstracting: an International Bibliography*, and *Indexing from A to Z*. He also contributes frequently to *Journal of the American Society for Information Science*, *The Indexer* and other professional journals.

Ralph Lee Woodward, Jr. is Professor of History at Tulane University, New Orleans. He is the author of *Central America, a Nation Divided*, 2nd ed. (1985), as well as several monographs and more than seventy scholarly articles on modern Latin America. He has also compiled volumes in the World Bibliographical Series on *Belize* (1980), *El Salvador* (1988), *Guatemala* (Rev. Ed.) (1992) and *Nicaragua* (Rev. Ed.) (1994). Dr. Woodward edited the Central American section of the *Research Guide to Central America and the Caribbean* (1985) and is currently associate editor of Scribner's *Encyclopedia of Latin American History*.

VOLUME 186

Slovenia

Cathie Carmichael

Compiler

CLIO PRESS
OXFORD, ENGLAND · SANTA BARBARA, CALIFORNIA
DENVER, COLORADO

British Library Cataloguing in Publication Data
Carmichael, Cathie
Slovenia. – (World Bibliographical series; vol. 186)
1. Slovenia – Bibliography
I. Title
016.9′4973

ISBN 1–85109–239–0

ABC-CLIO Ltd.,
Old Clarendon Ironworks,
35A Great Clarendon Street,
Oxford OX2 6AT, England.

———————

ABC-CLIO Inc.,
130 Cremona Drive,
Santa Barbara,
CA 93116, USA

Designed by Bernard Crossland.
Typeset by Columns Design and Production Services Ltd., Reading, England.
Printed and bound in Great Britain by Bookcraft (Bath) Ltd., Midsomer Norton.

THE WORLD BIBLIOGRAPHICAL SERIES

This series, which is principally designed for the English speaker, will eventually cover every country (and many of the world's principal regions), each in a separate volume comprising annotated entries on works dealing with its history, geography, economy and politics; and with its people, their culture, customs, religion and social organization. Attention will also be paid to current living conditions – housing, education, newspapers, clothing, etc.– that are all too often ignored in standard bibliographies; and to those particular aspects relevant to individual countries. Each volume seeks to achieve, by use of careful selectivity and critical assessment of the literature, an expression of the country and an appreciation of its nature and national aspirations, to guide the reader towards an understanding of its importance. The keynote of the series is to provide, in a uniform format, an interpretation of each country that will express its culture, its place in the world, and the qualities and background that make it unique. The views expressed in individual volumes, however, are not necessarily those of the publisher.

VOLUMES IN THE SERIES

Contents

Contents

Contents

Introduction

Any visitor to Slovenia will be struck by the variety of landscapes and ecology in this small Alpine republic with a population of approximately 2 million people. In the west, there is the limestone Karst, dry and harsh in the summer, and on the short coastline there are tiny Venetian-style harbours and salt-pans. To the north are the Karawanken Alps, tipped by snow for most of the year, and to the south the gentle green hills of Dolenjska. In the east, one finds the flatter landscape of the Pannonian plain stretching towards Hungary. There is also a corresponding degree of variation in climate from season to season, with Ljubljana shrouded in mists from the *Ljubljansko barje* in autumn, covered with snow in winter, fresh and wet in the spring and basking in Mediterranean-style sunshine in summer.

Yet in spite of the dramatic geographical variation within Slovenia, this country has an identity which is quite distinct, but, in turn, similar to its neighbours in Italy, Austria, Hungary and Croatia. Above all, what makes this small country a distinctive nation is the Slovene language, spoken by over 90 per cent of the population as a first language and used exclusively as the executive language of the republic. The Slovene language, like the landscape, varies enormously from valley to valley, especially in the Alps and as the Slovenes themselves say *'vsaka vas ima svoj glas'* ('every village has its own voice'). Despite its variety of dialects, since Slovene was first codified by Protestant reformers in the sixteenth century, it has been the strongest centripetal force in this region (except perhaps for Catholicism since the Slovenes were 're-converted' in the seventeenth century).

Although the Republic of Slovenia is a new political formation, the Slovenes have an old and distinct national culture. Proto-Slovenes moved into the Alps from about the sixth century onwards, covering a area which at its height stretched across the territory of contemporary Austria. After gradually losing their autonomy to their German neighbours, the Slovenes came under the control of the Habsburg dynasty in the Middle Ages. The vast majority of ethnic Slovenes thus remained as 'Austrians' until the dissolution of the Habsburg monarchy in 1918.

The Slovenes then embarked on other 'partnerships' with their neighbours to the South and were re-incorporated into Royalist Yugoslavia (1918-41), Austria or Italy and after the war into Communist Yugoslavia (1945-90), Austria or Italy. During most of this period, the Slovenes were 'Yugoslavians' as they had been 'Austrians' before – willing participants in the day-to-day running of the state but never at the cost of sacrificing their ethnic identity to more numerous neighbours. The Slovenian Republic of Yugoslavia declared itself independent on 25 June 1991 after a plebiscite on this issue six months earlier. After an uneasy war lasting ten days, the troops of the Yugoslav People's Army fought against the citizens of one of its own republics, but eventually lost the war of nerves and the wholesale backing of the international community. Since full-scale international recognition in the spring of 1992, Slovenia has had surprisingly little 'official' contact with its former Yugoslavian partners, other than to disagree with Croatia about border settlements and to house an influx of Bosnian refugees.

There has never been a better time for English-language readers to learn about the new Alpine republic, since English has largely displaced German as the main second language for publications about Slovenia in the last twenty years. The contents of this bibliography are aimed largely at the reader of English with access to libraries in the English-speaking world. Items in Slovene, German or Italian have been kept to a minimum, although further research will undoubtedly be greatly enhanced if the reader also has knowledge of these languages. In the bibliography, I use 'Slovene' to mean members of the *ethnos* that speak the Slovene language and 'Slovenian' to mean citizens of the Socialist Republic of Slovenia and its successor state the Republic of Slovenia. This usage may conflict with other English-language writers, especially in the United States of America. Eventually, like the term 'Italian', which corresponds both to ethnic and political descriptions, the term 'Slovenian' will become universal. At present, however, both adjectives still exist and I have tried to use both terms following the above criteria, without imputing any special value to either term.

Acknowledgements

As with any research project, the compilation of this bibliography leaves the author with many personal and professional debts to acknowledge. At ABC-CLIO, I am grateful for the assiduous advice of the series editor Robert Neville. John Allcock and John Horton have always been helpful and enthusiastic and I have greatly benefited from the fantastic library resources on the former Yugoslavia at Bradford University. At Middlesex University, Christine Bradford, the Librarian for History and Politics, has been an invaluable help to me.

At Ljubljana University, where I studied as a postgraduate student from 1989 to 1990, I was frequently assisted by Miha Bregant, Ljubica Črnivec, Metka Čuk, Božidar Jezernik, Janez Šumrada and Peter Vodopivec. During my regular return visits, I have also been most grateful for the company of Irena Watton, Deryn Verity, Mary Trimble, Mojca Ramšak, Glenda Sluga, James Gow, John Cox, Rajko and Andreja Muršič, Nick Oliver, Mark Thompson, Sanja Malbaša, Zmago Šmitek and Sara Sežun. Back in Britain, I have greatly benefited from conversations with Gerry Stone, who has done so much to promote the study of Slovene language and culture in this country.

At home, I am grateful to my family, particularly Patrick, John, Christina and Una for giving me support while undertaking this project. Patrick, with his vastly superior knowledge of information technology also helped me to compile the indexes. I dedicate this volume to all the above and to Jana Valenčič for her courageous work on behalf of the cause of Slovenian independence.

London
17th June 1995

The Country and Its People

1 **Slovenia in European affairs.**
John A. Arnez.   New York; Washington, DC: Studia Slovenica, 1958.
x, 204p.
A historical narrative of the Slovene people intended as an introduction for the non-specialist reader.

2 **Independent Slovenia: origins, movements, prospects.**
Edited by Jill Benderly, Evan Kraft.   London: Macmillan, 1994. 262p.
maps.
A collection of essays on history, politics and culture, which should be regarded as the major English-language work on Slovenia. One of the strengths of the collection must surely be the variety of political opinions expressed without losing the unity and national significance of the theme. Vlasta Jalušič (p. 135-57) discusses the links between gender and national politics in a comprehensive survey which, among other things, questions the role of the Catholic Church in Slovenia since independence, while Gregor Tomc considers youth culture and the 'politics of punk' (p. 113-34). Tonci Kuzmanić rejects 'the lacuna of both left and right explanations' of Slovenian independence by examining the role of trade unions (p. 159-79). Skilfully edited by a prominent peace activist (Benderly) and an economist (Kraft), the edition is the ideal point of departure for the reader who has no previous background in the subject.

3 **The Slovenes: a small nationality.**
Elizabeth Christitch.   *Month*, vol. 132 (1918), p. 415-21.
A summary of the religious and social position of the Slovenes after the First World War.

The Country and Its People

4 **This is Slovenia: a glance at the land and its people.**
Edited by Rudolf Čuješ. Toronto: Slovenian National Federation of
Canada, 1958. 221p. map. (Produced and distributed through the
Research Center for Slovenian Culture, Willowdale, Ontario. Publication,
no. 1).
An introduction to Slovenia intended for Canadian Slovenes.

5 **Slovenian heritage, Vol. 1.**
Edited by Edward Gobetz. Willoughby Hills, Ohio: Slovenian Research
Center of America, 1980. 642p.
Aimed at the children and grandchildren of American Slovenes, the book includes
portraits of prominent Slovenes, both in the New World and in Europe, as well as
translations of the poetry of Oton Župančič and France Prešeren and the prose of Ivan
Cankar. For biographical information about Gobetz, see his '35 years of research on
Slovenian heritage or how we confronted the woes of belonging to an unknown ethnic
group in America', *South Slav Journal*, vol. 11, no. 1 (Spring 1988), p. 22-32.

6 **Voices from the Slovene nation.**
Edited by Henry Huttenbach, Peter Vodopivec. *Nationalities Papers*,
vol. 21, no. 1 (Spring 1993). 200p.
This special book-length edition of the semi-annual journal published by the
Association for the Study of Nationalism of the USSR and Eastern Europe is entirely
dedicated to looking at Slovenian independence from different perspectives. The
geographer Ivan Gams writes that 'Yugoslavia has been the only European country to
join nations from the West on the one hand and from the border areas of Southeast and
Eastern Europe on the other. The result is evident: ethnic turmoil and general
discontent' (p. 26). Former Foreign Minister Dimitrij Rupel states his own case in
'Slovenia in post-modern Europe' (p. 51-60). 'In post-modern Europe, the concept of
a national state is giving way to inter-national and super-state combinations while in
line with its conservatism, it retains the content of national states, content which could
not in the past exist without a state framework. The Slovene national state will be a
temporary solution in European progress, and it will persist as long as other European
nation states. I have frequently stated that Slovenia is willing to renounce its
sovereignty to Brussels and Strasbourg, but not to Belgrade.' Are these prophetic
words written at a time of crisis; an incisive critique of pre-modern politics in former
Yugoslavia; or merely fine words to cloak Slovenian nationalism?

7 **Slovenia and the Slovenes.**
Anthony J. Klančar. *Journal of Central European Affairs*, vol. 6, no. 1
(April 1946), p. 1-20.
Klančar surveys some of the high points of Slovene culture from the Middle Ages
onwards and considers cultural developments in the twentieth century. An interesting
example of Slovenian Yugoslavism. For a similar contemporary account see also
Robert St John, 'These are the Slovenes' in his *The silent people speak* (New York:
Doubleday, 1948, p. 348-97).

2

8   **Brižinski spomeniki.** (The Freising fragments.)
    Edited by Janko Kos (et al.).   Ljubljana: Slovenska Akademija znanosti
    in umetnosti, 1993. 197p.

The Freising fragments, dating from the ninth century, are the oldest known Slavonic manuscript. In this book the original manuscript appears in photographic form and the edition also contains a full bibliography and dictionary of terms. In addition, there is an excellent English translation of the fragments (p. 121-9) provided by Gerald Stone. For a linguistic analysis of the fragments see Frederik H. H. Kortlandt, 'Jers and nasal vowels in the Freising fragments', *Slavistična revija*, vol. 23 (1975), p. 405-12.

9   **Les Slovènes.** (The Slovenes.)
    Ivan Krek, translated by A. U.   Paris: Felix Alcan, 1917. 85p.

Written to publicize the Slovene cause during the First World War, this general survey of Slovene history and culture is perhaps more informative about the politics of its time rather than about the putative subject matter.

10   **The making of modern Slovenia.**
    Archibald Lyall.   *Slavonic and East European Review*, vol. 17, no. 50
    (Jan. 1939), p. 404-15.

Writing just prior to the Second World War, Lyall gives a brief discussion of the 'highlights' of the history of the Slovenes, before discussing the role of Korošec's People's Party in royalist Yugoslavia. It is of interest to the contemporary reader that he writes: 'The Slovenes are in Jugoslavia and yet apart from it. They place the good of Slovenia first and last in all their calculations and it is not necessary to impute to them any very deep sentimental feeling for Jugoslavia as a whole . . .' (p. 415).

11   **The ethonym of the Slavs: common Slavic *slovene.**
    J. Peter Maher.   *Journal of Indo-European Studies*, vol. 2, no. 2
    (1974), p. 143-55.

Explores the etymology of the word 'Slovene' in 'Common Slavic'. On Indo-European linguistics see also Eric P. Hamp, 'Indo-European O-grade deverbal thematics in Slovene', *Slovene Studies*, vol. 10, no. 1 (1988), p. 65-70.

12   **Political and social conditions in the Slovene lands (Carniola, Carinthia, Illyrian littoral and Styria).**
    London: Nisbet, 1915-16. 36p. (The Southern Slav Library, vol. 6).

A survey of Slovene history issued during the politically sensitive war years and intended for a British audience.

13   **Slovenia's independence: a reversal of history.**
    Carole Rogel.   *Problems of Communism*, vol. 40, no. 4 (July-Aug.
    1991), p. 31-40.

Rogel considers the political developments that led to Slovenia's secession from Yugoslavia in the light of two hundred years of more or less pro-Yugoslav sentiment. She argues that Yugoslavism created Slovene national consciousness which was non existent before the late eighteenth century. The impulse to leave Yugoslavia, was created by short-term dissatisfaction (particularly with Slobodan Milošević over the Kosovo question), but also by unsatisfactory interpretations of Yugoslavist options by the Belgrade-dominated royalist Yugoslavia and by the Communists after the war.

14 Landscapes of Slovenia.
Jože Velikonja. *Slovene Studies*, vol. 11, no. 1/2 (1989), p. 137-46.

A rather poetical discussion of the relationship between man and environment in Slovenia, the 'creative tension' that always exists but which is rarely explored within 'positivist' parameters of research. Considering the limestone Karst, Velikonja writes 'the hardship of fragmented fields and rocky walls, the heavy reddish soil and the luxurious greenery of the maturing grapevines, the striking campanile of the local churches and the rich walls of the stone houses, the *kraška hisa*. Hidden clusters of houses in a shallow valley in the rugged landscape, or perched on top of a hill as at Stanjel or Vrabce: the human landscape shows the roughness of the land: shake hands with any of the inhabitants and their rough palm will remind you of the scarred surface of the eroded land. People here more than elsewhere, are part of the land. Without them the land would vanish: their livelihood would be carried away through the dissected surface which does not hold water. Storms would wash away the white outcrops: half an hour after a storm no evidence remains of any rain, other than the freshness of the air and the revived greenery of the thorny bushes' (p. 141). Who could resist that?

15 La Repubblica della Slovenia tra l'Europa e i Balcani. (The Republic of Slovenia between Europe and the Balkans.)
Egidio Vrsaj. Milan, Italy: Franco Angeli, 1993. 188p. (Series collana dell'Istituto di sociologia internationale, Gorizia, I.S.I.G., no. 18).

A survey of recent political developments from a Slovene perspective.

Geography

General

16   Mountains of Slovenia.
France Berne, Matjaž Kmecl.   Ljubljana: Cankarjeva založba, 1989.
326p.
This full-colour guide to the Alps in Slovenia includes the Julian range along the Italian border and the Karawanken mountains along the Austrian border. Matjaž Kmecl is also the author of *On the sunny side of the Alps*, translated by Roger Metcalfe (Ljubljana: Ministry of Tourism and Catering, Gorenjski tisk, Kranj, 1992. 30p.); and more recently, *Slovenian mountain fairy tale*, translated by Amidas (Ljubljana: Mihelač, 1994. 190p.). All three books offer a splendid photographic introduction to the Slovenian Alps.

17   Slowenien: ein neuer europaeischer Staat. (Slovenia: a new European state.)
H. Bueschenfeld.   *Geographische Rundschau*, no. 44 (1992), p. 716-23.
The author assesses the future prospects for Slovenia, particularly in the light of a decline in industrialization and rising unemployment. He also examines some aspects of urbanization.

18   Die Ehre dess Herzogthums Crain. (The glory of the Duchy of Carniola.)
Johann Weikhard von Valvasor.   Laybach [Ljubljana]: Wolfgang Moritz Endter, 1689. 3,532p. 4 vols.
An outstanding example of seventeenth-century topography and ethnography from a native of Ljubljana. Valvasor corresponded with the Royal Society in London and produced this magnificent work to publicize his native Carniola (Kranj) to the outside world. For a comprehensive biography of the Carniolan polymath with an English-

language summary (p. 385-417), see Branko Reisp, *Janez Vajkard Valvasor* (Ljubljana: Mladinska knjiga, 1983. 431p.).

Regional

19 **Land utilisation in the Karst region of Zgornja Pivka, Slovenia.**
Paul B. Alexander. New York: Studia Slovenica, 1967. 132p. maps. bibliog.

A historical and geographical study of the Zgornja Pivka area in the limestone Karst, looking in particular at such problems as transport routes for transhumance and changes in the land use such as the decline of the autochthonous deciduous trees and the plantation of conifers from the nineteenth century onwards.

20 **The regions of Slovenia.**
Svetozar Ilešič. *Geographia Polonica*, vol. 36 (1977), p. 73-82.

Traces the history of Slovenian regional geography from the work of its founder, Anton Melik (1890-1966). Ilešič then discusses the five main ecological regions of Slovenia, as well as its five main regional units, which differ somewhat in that they take economic and political factors into consideration. A basic introduction from one of Slovenia's finest twentieth-century geographers. See also Ilešič's 'The regional socio-economic structure of the Socialist Republic of Slovenia', *Geografische Tijdschrift*, vol. 5, no. 4 (Sept. 1971), p. 485-90.

21 **The village of Seboborci on the Slovenian fringes of the Great Pannonian Plain.**
Vladimir Klemenčič. *Geographia Polonica*, no. 5 (1969), p. 215-34.

Klemenčič looks at the ethnic and economic characteristics of a village in the Magyar–Slovene border area. Of related interest is his 'The village of Podgorje in the Slovenian sub-Alpine region', *Geographia Polonica*, no. 2 (1965), p. 195-278.

22 **The Upper Soča valley.**
A. E. Moodie, G. Joan Fuller, Monica M. Cole, G. J. Butland.
Geographical Studies, vol. 2, no. 2 (1955), p. 63-110.

The report of a team of 36 British geographers who visited the Soča valley in August 1953 under the auspices of the Geographical Field Group. In the study, the authors describe the physical background, settlement and population, land utilization and the agrarian economy. They conclude with a detailed study of transhumance. The report includes photographs taken by the team, maps and diagrams.

23 **The Triglav National Park In the 1980s.**
Fred Singleton. *Slovene Studies*, vol. 10, no. 1 (1988), p. 39-49.

Considers the history of the Triglav National Park, which expanded to cover some 210,000 acres of the Julian Alps in 1981. Triglav even has its own species of flora, the

Triglavska roža, which leads Singleton to express concern about the preservation of its natural beauty.

24   **Slovene studies: being studies carried out by members of the Le Play Society in the Alpine valleys of Slovenia (Yugoslavia).**
Edited by L. Dudley Stamp.   London: Le Play Society, 1933. 70p. maps.
A British geographical study of the Solčava valley in the Karawanken Alps, undertaken by members of the the Le Play Society, which includes observations on the local ecology and *čebelarstvo* (bee-keeping), and a collection of fascinating photographs. Almost forty years later the Brathay Exploration Group organized two expeditions to the Solčava, in order to record the changes that had taken place. The results were published as *Slovene studies 1971 and 1972*, edited by David Boardman (Ambleside, England: Brathay Hall Trust, 1973. 62p.).

25   **Internal migration in Slovenia 1961-1971.**
Colin Thomas.   *Geografski vestnik*, vol. 48 (1976), p. 77-92.
Reviews how and why people moved within the Republic of Slovenia during a period of relative economic prosperity and freedom of movement.

26   **Population mobility in frontier communities: examples from the Julian March 1931-1945.**
Colin Thomas.   *Transactions of the Institute of British Geographers* (new series), vol. 4, no. 1 (1979), p. 44-61.
A study of 21 rural settlements in the Idrija area, which was incorporated into Italy after the First World War, but integrated into Slovenia after 1945. Under the Italian administration, population registration took place through the 1931 and 1936 censuses which, in theory, 'permit . . . the reconstruction of the population composition by age, sex, marital status, occupation, birth place, former residence in the present community, together with cross-tabulation of any pairs of the variables'. The value of the records declined during the war, due to other dislocations. Thomas then proceeds to analyse this basic data for the settlements (Table 1, p. 49) along age and marriage lines.

27   **Alpine communities in transition.**
Colin Thomas, M. Vojvoda.   *Geography*, vol. 58, pt. 3 (July 1973), p. 217-26.
Basing their account on fieldwork carried out in Srednja vas in the the Bohinj basin in 1967 and published statistics from 1953-71, the authors present a picture of a rural community coming under increasing influence from outside. Patterns of cattle transhumance in the Alps, seen by many geographers as typical examples of a traditional economy, have changed greatly in the twentieth century, especially since 1945. The Bohinj basin has been affected both by out-migration to the towns and by tourism. The article draws on examples from other research carried out in Slovenia and is therefore a good example in English of the wealth of material that has been published in Slovene in the periodicals *Geografski zbornik* (Annals of Geography) and *Geografski vestnik* (Geographical Journal). These annual periodicals are now publishing material in English with Slovene summaries.

Political

28   **Geographical problems of frontier regions: the case of the Italo-Yugoslav border landscape.**
Vladimir Klemenčič, Milan Bufon. In: *The geography of border landscapes.* Edited by D. Rumley, J. V. Minghi. London: Routledge, 1991, p. 86-103.
Surveys the problems that have marked Italo-Yugoslavian bilateral relations up to the time of Slovenian independence.

29   **Cultural elements of integration and transformation of border regions – the case of Slovenia.**
Vladimir Klemenčič, Milan Bufon. *Political Geography*, vol. 13, no. 1 (Jan. 1994), p. 73-83.
Argues that the Slovenes are peculiarly interested in the topic of border regions and that 'Slovenia in its entirety could be characterised as a border region' (p. 73). This is in part because of historical factors that have fragmented the Eastern Alps and in part because of ethnic questions. The article includes a map of the transport infrastructure of Slovenia and its neighbourhood, illustrating state borders, ethnic minorities (Hungarians, Italians) within the Slovene borders and Slovene minority populations in Italy, Austria and Hungary (p. 74). The nature of Slovenia's border led the authors to speculate on the 'standard theory of the centre–periphery relation' (p. 81).

30   **Gorica (The geographical basis of its foundation).**
Anton Melik. Ljubljana: Research Institute for Frontier Questions, 1946. 21p. maps.
A study of the ethnic frontier between Italy and Slovenia, in an area where the frontier was redrawn after the Second World War.

31   **The Italo-Yugoslav boundary: a study in political geography.**
Arthur E. Moodie. London: Philip, 1945. 241p. maps. bibliog.
A historical and geographical study of the Julian March which has been the subject of bitter political disputes throughout the twentieth century, and subject to several major territorial divisions during the same period.

32   **Some new border problems in the Julian March.**
Arthur E. Moodie. *Transactions of the Institute of British Geographers*, vol. 16 (1950), p. 83-93.
Discusses the geographical impact of the Treaty of Paris of February 1947, which defined the new boundary between Italy and Yugoslavia and that of the Free Territory of Trieste. Redrawing the boundaries of 1920 had an economic impact during peacetime and Moodie discusses in particular the boundary between Goriška brda (in Slovenia), which was and remains an extensive fruit-growing region and Gorizia in Italy. From a geographical and agricultural point of view, Moodie considered the 'new boundary a well-nigh insurmountable barrier as is well illustrated by the extremely irksome formalities associated with travel and currency facilities between the two countries' (p. 93).

33 **From Koper to Piran.**
    Zvone Petek, Salvator Žitko, translated by Milan Mlačnik. Ljubljana:
    Mladinska knjiga, 1986. 159p.
The Republic of Slovenia has a tiny littoral sandwiched between Trieste and Croatian
Istria. This fabulously illustrated guide shows all the towns of 'Slovenian Istria' in
full-colour photographs, particularly Koper, Izola, Piran, and the resort of Portorož.

34 **Geography and ethnicity: geografija in narodnosti.**
    Marjan Ravbar. Ljubljana: Inštitut za geografijo, Ljubljana University,
    1993. 299p. maps. (Geografica Slovenica series, vol. 24).
A detailed study of the relationship between geographical terrain and ethnic
(i.e., linguistic) groups in the Eastern Alps region. The text is in English and Slovene.

35 **Ports and politics in Yugoslavia.**
    Dennison I. Rusinow. New York: American Universities Field Staff,
    1964. 23p.
The importance of ports in Yugoslavian politics has never been neglected, particularly
in the case of Trieste. Here Rusinow looks at other cases including that of Koper,
which became the main sea outlet for the Socialist Republic of Slovenia after the
Second World War and remains so today.

36 **The port of Koper.**
    Milenko Sober. Koper, Slovenia: Port Authority, 1985. 159p.
Before the twentieth century, Koper (Capodistria) had a strong Venetian-Italian
influence, which left its mark on the architectural style of the town. Its primary
importance after the war was as a port which catered for both commercial and trading
vessels, although it also attracted tourists and water sports enthusiasts. For a survey of
continuing maritime trade in Slovenia and Croatia since the break-up of Yugoslavia,
see Ivan Berenyi, 'Against the odds', *Seatrade Review*, vol. 22, no. 3 (March 1993),
p. 6-11.

Economic

37 **Aspects of the development of capitalism in Yugoslavia: the role of
    the state in the formation of a satellite economy.**
    John B. Allcock. In: *An historical geography of the Balkans.* Edited
    by F. W. Carter. London, New York: Academic Press, 1977,
    p. 535-80.
Applies the ideas on development of André Gunder Frank to Yugoslavia, looking in
some detail at the relationship between the development of the Slovene economy
within the Habsburg monarchy. In the same volume see also F. W. Carter, 'Urban
development in the Western Balkans 1200-1800' (p. 147-95), which covers the history
of Slovene towns and is illustrated with maps.

Special features

38 **The fertility of Lake Cerknica.**
Cathie Carmichael. *Social History*, vol. 19, no. 3 (Oct. 1994),
p. 305-17.
This article argues that the scientific discourses within the Royal Society during the
late seventeenth and eighteenth centuries, in particular about the fertile nature of Lake
Cerknica (Sl. Cerkniško jezero), drew upon older peasant knowledge about the Karst
area, which is now part of Slovenia. Writers who have discussed the popular culture of
East-Central Europe have talked about a 'geographical complex' where ritualistic
beliefs about fertility existed until recent times. The existence of these two levels of
knowledge has lead the author to speculate whether Lake Cerknica had any wider
geographical significance at the level of popular culture.

39 **Geological development in Slovenia and Croatia.**
Edited by Katica Drobne. Ljubljana: Slovenska akademija znanosti in
umetnosti, 1979. 258p. map.
Geology was an important science in the former Yugoslavia, due in part to the legacy
of the Serb geographer Jovan Cvijić in the early twentieth century, but also due to the
extensive research undertaken on the geomorphology of the Dinaric Karst. This study
gives a sample of important work carried out in the two northern republics.

40 *Periculina slovenica*, **B. form, from the Paleocene of Majevica Mt.
(Yugoslavia) and the new family Fabulariidae.**
Katica Drobne. Ljubljana: Slovenska akademija znanosti in umetnosti,
1984. 32p.
Describes the fossil *Periculina slovenica*, which the author first described in Slovenia
in 1974 and a new form that she subsequently discovered in Bosnia, the
'B-form'. The text is in English with a Slovene summary, and there are eight leaves of
plates.

41 **Mineral deposits in Permian and Triassic beds of Slovenia.**
Matija Drovenik. In: *Mineral deposits of the Alps and of the Alpine
epoch in Europe.* Edited by Hans J. Schneider. Berlin: Springer,
1983, p. 88-96.
Drovenik describes research into the distribution and nature of mineral deposits in the
Alpine areas of Slovenia.

42 **Some morphological features of the Dinaric Karst.**
Ivan Gams. *Geographical Journal*, vol. 135, no. 4 (Dec. 1969),
p. 563-72.
Describes the main landscape features of the Karst areas of the former Yugoslavia and
discusses the relevant scientific literature. Gams also includes a list of commercialized
and other caves and potholes for all the republics of former Yugoslavia – indicating
whether they are wet or dry or a combination, and whether they have known
archaeological sites. The article includes two figures: one of the locations of the caves

(including a detailed inset of the area around Postojna); and the second illustrating Karst *polja* (valleys) in the former Yugoslavia, nine of which were in Slovenia. For further details on Slovenia, see Gams's 'Speleological characteristics of the Slovene Karst', *Naše jame*, vol. 7, no. 1/2 (1965), p. 41-50.

43 **Slovenska kraška terminologija/Slovene Karst terminology.**
Edited by Ivan Gams. Ljubljana: Zveza geografskih institucij Jugoslavije, 1973. 76p.
This technical dictionary which translates Slovene terms for the Karst landscape into English terms is useful for specialist geomorphologists.

44 **The delimination and characteristics of the Alps in Slovenia.**
Ivan Gams. *Geographica Iugoslavica*, vol. 5 (1984), p. 7-14.
A summary of research on the Slovene Alps and a description of their characteristics. Of related interest is Milan Šifrer, 'The main results of the geomorphological research of the Slovene Alpine area', *Geographica Iugoslavica*, vol. 5 (1984). p. 24-30.

45 **Speleological characterisics of Alpine Karst in Slovenia, northwestern Yugoslavia.**
Andrej Kranjc. *Norsk Geografisk Tidsskrift*, vol. 38 (1984), p. 177-83.
Describes the Karst landscape to the north-west of Ljubljana, an area which has mixed geomorphological characteristics.

46 **Guidelines and procedures used to eliminate the impact of earthquake in the Soča valley.**
Anton Ladava. In: *Social and economic aspects of earthquakes.* Ljubljana; Ithaca, New York: Institute for Testing and Research in Materials and Structures, 1982, p. 413-23.
This volume contains the proceedings of the Third International Conference for the Social and Economic Aspects of Earthquakes and Planning to Mitigate their Impacts which took place in Bled in 1981. Ladava's paper examines the measures to prevent earthquake damage in the wake of the Friulian disaster of 1976. See also M. O. Adamič, 'Classification of earthquake prone areas on the basis of potential damage in Slovenia, Yugoslavia', *Ekistics*, vol. 51 (1984), p. 536-9.

47 **Double inversion over the Bohinj valley.**
Zdravko Petkovšek. *Weather*, vol. 15, no. 4 (April 1960), p. 131-6.
Petkovšek explains the topographical and weather conditions that made a temperature inversion over Lake Bohinj on 30 January 1959, when there was a 'fog sea' over the valleys and lowlands of the Southeastern Alps. The work includes illustrations, and incredible photographs taken by the author.

48 **The Quaternary development of the Dravinja hills (NE Slovenia) and of the neighbouring fringe lands.**
Milan Šifrer. *Geografski zbornik*, vol. 14 (1974), p. 172-7.
Reviews the recent development of landforms and rivers in the hills bordering Dravska polje near Maribor. For a more geographically extensive study of Quaternary conditions in Slovenia, which concentrates on vegetation development in response to climatic change, see also Metka Čuliberg, *Late glacial vegetation in Slovenia* (Ljubljana: Slovenska akademija znanosti in umetnosti, 1991. 52p.).

49 **Karst landforms.**
Marjorie M. Sweeting. London: Macmillan, 1972. 362p.
A comprehensive survey of research into different types of limestone Karst from Jamaica to Slovenia, which includes a great deal of information about the 'Classical Karst' from Trieste to Ljubljana. Slovene technical terms for Karst landforms, such as *uvala* and *polje*, are also explained.

50 **Local wind *bora*.**
Masatoshi M. Yoshino. Tokyo: University of Tokyo Press, 1976. 289p.
The *burja* or *bora* wind characterically whistles across the western Karst area of Slovenia coming in from the Adriatic. This scientific study measures its intensity and effects. The papers are written in English or German, with abstracts in English.

Maps, atlases and gazetteers

51 **Atlas Slovenije: 109 preglednih kart v merilu 1:50,000 in Slovenija v sliki in besedi.** (Atlas of Slovenia: 109 maps on the scale 1:50,000 and Slovenia in pictures and words.)
Ljubljana: Mladinska knjiga za Geodetski zavod Slovenije, 1986. 365p.
A beautifully produced, large-format atlas of Slovenia, with text describing special features and including 180 photographs.

52 **Ethnological cartography and atlases.**
Branimir Bratanić. In: *Europe as a cultural area*. Edited by J. Cuisenier. The Hague: Mouton, 1979, p. 105-22.
These are ethnographic maps of former Yugoslavia, including Slovenia, and particularly concentrating on agricultural zones and the implements used.

53 **Ljubljana: maps, tourist guide, information.**
Edited by Marjan Krušič, translated by Milan Mlačnik. Ljubljana:
Mladinska knjiga za Geodetski zavod Slovenije, 1993. 119p.

A pocket-sized guide to Ljubljana, which includes 59 pages of maps, a brief
chronological survey, some suggested out-of-town excursions, and a guided walk
through the city. Ideal for the tourist and local alike, especially as it includes an index
of street names.

54 **Slowenien: Karte und Fuehrer.** (Slovenia: map and guide.)
Augustin Lah (et al.). Vienna: Freytag-Berndt und Artaria, 1994.

This well-produced and widely distributed colour map of Slovenia is on a scale of
1:125,000. It comes with a brief guide to the most touristic areas, and a glossary of
town names.

55 **Atlas linguistique pour servir à l'étude du duel en Slovène.**
(Linguistic atlas of dual usage in Slovene.)
Lucien Tesnière. Paris: Champion, 1925. 39p.

The dual is an archaic linguistic form that survives in some dialects of Slovene and is
enshrined in contemporary standard Slovene. This atlas indicates the geographical
spread of this form which is used in Ljubljana, has an entirely different form in
Styrian dialects, and does not occur at all in Triestine Slovene. For further details, see
also his *Les formes du duel en Slovène* (The forms of the dual in Slovene) (Paris:
Champion, 1925. 454p.).

Tourism and Travel Guides, Sports and Recreation

56 **The development of the Triglav National Park, Slovenia.**
J. Alan Coley.   Bradford, England: University of Bradford,
Postgraduate School of Yugoslav Studies, 1985. 48p. 8 maps. (Bradford
Studies on Yugoslavia, no. 8).

The Triglav National Park, which covers a large area of the north-east of Slovenia was
established in 1961, but gained more land after 1981. This study, part of a detailed
series produced by the Postgraduate School of Research Studies at Bradford
University (now renamed the Research Unit for Southeastern European Studies) looks
at the challenges of running this vast park, with particular regard to planning,
resources, and the concern that the Slovenes have for their environment. Coley
examines the problems associated with hydroelectric projects and tourism.

57 **Julian Alps: mountain walking and outline climbing guide.**
Compiled by Robin G. Collomb, assisted by M. Anderson.   Goring,
England: West Col Productions, 1978. 136p. maps.

The guide is intended for serious walkers and climbers. It shows basic accommodation
in mountain huts and mountain pathways, and provides translations of some basic
Slovene terms. It also includes a climber's guide to Triglav and other peaks of the
Julian range.

58 **Beautiful mountains: in the Yugoslav Alps.**
Fanny S. Copeland, illustrated by Edo Deržaj.   Split, Yugoslavia:
Jugoslav Bureau, 1931. 120p.

Fanny Copeland, English eccentric and erstwhile resident of the Slon Hotel, is still
remembered with affection as a great promoter of Slovene culture and the Yugoslav
cause at the Paris Peace conference in 1918-19. Her translations from Slovene into
English and her prolific work on Slovene popular culture led her to take an academic
post in Ljubljana University in the interwar period. This book is both an elegy for the
Slovenian Alps and a guide for the tourist.

14

59 **A short guide to the Slovene Alps (Jugoslavia) for British and American tourists.**
Fanny S. Copeland, M. Debelkova.   Ljubljana: Kleinmayr and Bamberg, 1936. 127p.
One of the finest pre-war guides to the Eastern Alps within the Yugoslavian frontier (the Julian Alps came under Italian jurisdiction in the interwar period). See also Fanny S. Copeland, 'Lost world in Carniola', *The Alpine Journal*, vol. 52, no. 260 (May 1940), p. 90-6.

60 **Lippizzaner: the story of the horses of Lipica.**
Milan Dolenc.   St Paul, Minnesota: Control Data Arts, 1981. 216p.
In 1580 the Habsburg authorities established a stud farm in the Karst, where horses imported from the Iberian peninsula were bred. The stables survived the subsequent changes in administration, and tourists now flock to see the beautiful white horses, known still by the German name of Lippizaners. For a shorter introduction see Zika Jovanović, 'The white horses of Lipica', *Yugoslav Review*, no. 1/2 (1986), p. 20-9.

61 **A guide to the Triglav National Park.**
Editor-in-chief Ivan Fabjan.   Bled, Slovenia: Natural Sciences Society of Slovenia/Triglav National Park, 1987. 270p. maps.
A comprehensive guide to the Triglav National Park, including suggested walks. It also offers detailed background material on the local culture, flora and fauna.

62 **The urban growth and spacial problems of recreation in Slovenia (Yugoslavia).**
Anton Gosar.   In: *Studies in the geography of tourism and recreation II.* Edited by Karl A. Sinnhuber, Felix Juelg.   Vienna: Verlag Ferdinand Hirt, 1979, p. 177-85. (Wiener Geographische Schriften, no. 53/54).
As the farming population was only one-sixth of the total Slovenian population at the time of the survey, demand for recreation for town-dwellers was particularly high when compared to the rest of Yugoslavia. Gosar identifies three main centres for leisure-time activities: urban centres (Maribor, Ljubljana and Celje), the Alps (Bohinj, Bled, Kranjska gora and Trenta) and the littoral (Koper and Western Istria). He presents data on distances and the duration of trips, as well as motives (i.e. sunbathing, picking mushrooms, skiing). Map 1 (p. 184-5) illustrates the main areas for tourism in Slovenia. In the same volume, in 'The Karst province of Trieste' (p. 143-6), Giovanna Giaretta assesses the impact of tourism along the Italo-Yugoslavian border (nowadays the border with Slovenia) and the impact of local laws protecting the environment which were proposed in 1971.

63 **Some characteristics of tourism in Slovenia.**
Anton Gosar.   *Slovene Studies*, vol. 12, no. 1 (1990), p. 33-42.
In Slovenia, 'a number of European macro-regions come into contact', so that the Republic has a varied landscape and offers a wide variety of recreation to the would-be tourist. Gosar analyses the basic characteristics of tourism in Slovenia, including the most frequently visited *občine* (municipal communes).

64 **The Postojna caves and other tourist caves in Slovenia.**
France Habe, translated by Rado Torkar, Vivienne Torkar. Postojna, Slovenia: Zavod postojnske jame, 1986. 4th ed. 104p. map. bibliog.
Although legends about the Karstic underworld existed for centuries in the popular culture of the Karst, the Postojna caves were not fully charted and explored until the mid-nineteenth century, which is chronicled here. Nowadays the spectacular caves are one of the most popular destinations for day trips in Slovenia. This guide offers a geological background to the underground limestone as well as a colour map of the main caves in this part of the Karst. For the more geological detail, see Alfred Šerko and Ivan Michler, *The caves of Postojna and other curiosities of the Karst* (Postojna: Zavod postojnske jame, 1952. 196p.).

65 **Secondary holiday lodgings in Slovenia and Western Istria.**
M. Jeršič. *Geografski vestnik*, vol. 4 (1968), p. 53-67.
Unlike many Western Europeans, Slovenes maintain strong links with the countryside, either through relatives or by owning property. This article looks at the ownership and locations of *wikendice* or weekend cottages.

66 **Bled.**
Joze Kastelič. Ljubljana: Slovenska akademija znanosti in umetnosti, 1948. 103p.
A guide to the early history, archaeology and anthropology of Slovenia's most popular resort, which has been an established destination for holidaymakers since the late nineteenth century.

67 **Ljubljana.**
Matjaž Kmecl. Ljubljana: Motovun, 1987. 173p.
Fabulously illustrated with full-colour photography, this 'coffee-table'-format book also provides a historical and cultural introduction to Ljubljana through the seasons. A brief warning: even the housing estates are photographed so as to look heavenly!

68 **Plečnik's Ljubljana.**
Peter Krečič, translated by Martin Cregreen. Ljubljana: Cankarjeva založba, 1991. 80p. maps.
Among the great 'gifts' of the architect Jože Plečnik (1872-1957) to the Slovenian nation were the wonderful buildings that he designed for Ljubljana, including the pink and grey stone National and University Library, finished in 1941, and the 'three bridges' (Tromostovje) that cross the Ljubljanica. This intricate pocket-sized guide is the perfect introduction to the architect himself and to the city that inspired him.

69 **Kamnik.**
Janez Majcenović, translated into English by Henka Skrlj. Kamnik, Slovenia: Komenda Lubadar, 1991. 144p.
Kamnik is one of the most beautiful towns in the Slovenian Alps, easily accessible from Ljubljana. This guide includes summaries in English, German and Italian.

70 Nova Gorica.
Branko Marušič.   Kranj, Slovenia: Gorenjski tisk, Motovun, 1988.
144p.

A brief illustrated guide to the history and culture of this intriguing town, which was 'partitioned' between Yugoslavia and Italy after the Second World War. Nova Gorica refers to the Slovenian town, whereas the Italians call their part simply Gorizia. Marušič has the advantage of being the leading historian of this area and an unrivalled authority.

71 Welcome in Slovenia: land and people.
Mitja Meršol.   Kranj, Slovenia: Gorenjski tisk, Motovun, 1988. 96p.

This basic pocket-sized guide-book offers the tourist a short historical introduction to Slovenia, and to some of the treasures of peasant culture as well as to art, music and literature. It is packed with facts and figures and contains many excellent colour photographs.

72 Ljubljana.
Nace Šumi.   Belgrade: NIP; Florence, Italy: SCALA, 1975. 183p.

An illustrated introduction to this beautiful city, from one of Slovenia's foremost cultural commentators.

Travellers' Accounts

73 **The native's return: an American immigrant visits Yugoslavia and discovers his old country.**
Louis Adamič.   New York: Harper, 1934. 370p. Reprinted Westport, Connecticut: Greenwood, 1975.

After emigrating to America as a very young man just before the First World War, Adamič returned to the Slovenian highlands of his youth as well as other parts of royalist Yugoslavia. Not only is this an interesting piece of autobiography, but it is also a valuable ethnographic source, as Adamič described many of the folk customs of his native village.

74 **A tale of five cities: life in provincial Europe today.**
John Ardagh.   London: Secker and Warburg, 1979. 457p.

Ljubljana is favourably compared to other small European towns in chapter six of this book (p. 375-437). A fascinating read for all those who have experienced the 'magic' of this wonderful place, particularly as Ardagh's account predates the 'cultural revolution' in the 1980s.

75 **A tour through Italy, Sicily, Istria, Carniola, the Tyrol and Austria in 1814.**
T. Baring.   London: Gale and Fenner, 1817. 268p.

This account, which covers both Istria and the western part of Slovenia, is generally positive, particularly as Baring noticed how few friars there were for a Catholic country. Travelling towards Ljubljana from the west, he remarked that 'the soil is good: and as the inhabitants have not multiplied so fast as to make it necessary to cut down the large forests of pine, of fir, of larch, of beech and of oak growing as nature planted them, intermixed with one another, and by turns forming separate clusters of their own species, your curiosity is continually gratified. Frequently, a small white chapel with a spiral steeple peeped from amongst the trees, while mountains of snow formed the background'. Thankfully, much of this countryside is unchanged today.

76 **A Brief Account of some Travels in Hvngaria, Servia, Bvlgaria, Macedonia, Thessaly, Avstria, Styria, Carinthia, Carniola and Friuli.**
Edward Brown. London: Benj. Tooke, 1673. 144p.

The earliest known publication of an English-speaking traveller in Slovenia. Edward Brown(e), a member of the Royal Society, described his journeys to Cerknica, Idrija and Zollfeld in Carinthia to see the ducal stone. In the absence of a guide-book, he reported that 'at Labach [Ljubljana], I happily met with Mr Tosh a Scotch apothecary in that town, who was very civil unto me, informing me of the places about and showing me many curiosities, and the several minerals of those parts' (p. 126).

77 **A journey in Carniola, Italy and France in the years 1817 and 1818.**
W. A. Cadell. Edinburgh: Archibald Constance and Co., 1820. 554p.

A hotch-potch of observations about the Slovene lands and other parts of Central Europe, which is curious because of its apparent ethnographic distance. Cadell discusses languages and agriculture – but not the people who undertook the tasks. Of particular interest is his description of the horizontal screens for drying buckwheat and the barns used for storing Indian corn (p. 24-5). He also mentions the cultivation of gourds, which will be a familiar sight nowadays to anyone who has travelled in Slovenia, as they often decorate the outside of houses, especially to the south-west of Ljubljana.

78 **Two gentlemen travellers in the Slovene lands in 1737.**
Catherine D. Carmichael. *Slovene Studies*, vol. 13, no. 1 (1991), p. 19-26.

When Richard Pococke travelled the Levant in the 1730s he took with him Jeremiah Milles, who recorded his travels in the form of letters to the Bishop of Waterford. This article discusses not only the itinerary that the two men took though the Slovene lands, but also their observations, particularly about the periodic Lake Cerknica.

79 **Halley in Istria.**
A. J. Cook. *Journal of Navigation*, vol. 37, no. 1 (1984), p. 1-23.

Edmond Halley, the astronomer and mathematician, travelled to the port of Trieste and the Istrian littoral on Imperial Commission in 1703 to look at the suitability of the different ports in the region. He left a number of comments about his trip in his notebooks and letters, which Cook discusses in this innovative article.

80 **The Dolomite Mountains. Excursions through Tyrol, Carinthia, Carniola and Friuli in 1861, 1862 and 1863.**
Josiah Gilbert, G. C. Churchill. London: Longman, Roberts and Green, 1864. 576p.

This account of the northern parts of present-day Slovenia contains a great deal of material about the local geology. It is instructive to note how visitors during the nineteenth century took far more interest in the Alps than their eighteenth-century predecessors, particularly in Mount Triglav (which was originally popularized by the naturalized Breton, Balthasar Hacquet). The authors considered Lake Bled (Veldes) to be 'the gem of Carniola', but were less enamoured with the 'dreadful' Slovene language, 'all k's and z's' (p. 290)!

19

81 An American visitor to the Idrija mercury mine in 1866.

Toussaint Hočevar. *Slovene Studies*, vol. 3, no. 1 (1981), p. 20-3.

A brief note about an American mining engineer, Mr C. E. Hartley, who was interested in the square-type furnace used in the mines in Slovenia. The California mine of New Idria began producing mercury in 1854 and the visit may thus represent 'a case of mid-19th century technology transfer from Slovenia to the United States' (p. 20).

82 Travels through Germany, Bohemia, Hungary, Switzerland, Italy and Lorrain, Vol. III.

John George Keyssler. London: A. Linde and T. Field, 1756. 385p.

This witty, slightly unconventional account of a journey across Europe, taking in parts of Western Slovenia and Istria, was written by a Hanoverian member of the Royal Society. Keyssler included his visit to the periodic Lake Cerknica where he recounted that the local inhabitants fished *tous nus*, while young monks hid behind bushes to watch. The journey is continued briefly in Volume IV (p. 1-10), where he found that in Ljubljana the 'peasants' wives roar out their Sclavonian hymns' on Corpus Christi day.

83 Alpine pilgrimage.

Julius Kugy, translated by Henry E. G. Tyndale. London: Murray, 1934. 368p. maps.

'Classic' account of travels in the Julian Alps written largely in 1918 by a Triestine, which includes observations on Slovene mythology and culture. The volume includes the author's own beautiful photographs.

84 On the shores of the Mediterranean.

Eric Newby. London: Pan in association with Collins, 1985. 448p.

Eric Newby married a Slovene, Wanda, after meeting her during the Second World War in Italy. The story of their meeting is retold movingly in *Love and war in the Apennines* (Harmondsworth: Penguin, 1978. 298p.). In the 'Mediterranean' volume, Newby recounts (in his typically droll style) a visit to his relatives in the Karst, where he waits for hours for a chicken to be killed during a local version of the wake.

85 A Description of the East, Vol. II, Part II.

Richard Pococke. London: W. Bowyer, 1745. 308p.

An encyclopaedic study of the Levant by Pococke whose portrait in oriental costume, including a turban, hangs in the Musée d'Art et d'Histoire in Geneva. Chapter 11, 'Of the county of Goritia and the Duchy of Carniola' (p. 257-62), contains descriptions of Lake Cerknica, Ajdovščina, Ljubljana and Idrija. In Chapter 10 (p. 255-7), Pococke recounts his visit to the 'Kaiserstool', around which the inaugural ceremonies of the dukes of Carinthia took place.

86   **A stroll to Syracuse.**
Johann Gottfried Seume, translated from the German by Alexander
Henderson, Elizabeth Henderson.   London: Oswald Wolff, 1964. 256p.

A straightforward but readable account of a journey across Europe, originally
published in German as *Spaziergang nach Syrakus im Jahre 1802* (Leipzig, 1803).
Travelling from Graz to Trieste via Ljubljana, Seume visited the caves of Postojna,
but evidently before the advent of mass tourism. 'As you can imagine I wanted to visit
the grotto, but it was difficult to find anyone to accompany me. At last a man from the
customs came with me . . . You can understand that I felt somewhat uneasy at
creeping about in the gorges looking for a grotto in Carniola, all alone with a complete
stranger, a man as strong as an ox . . . At last, after a lot of searching and losing our
way we came after half an hour to the entrance of the grotto. This is really romantic,
wild and uncanny, in a deep cauldron, with great rocks all round and overgrown with
the thickest pine forest' (p. 43).

87   **Louis Adamič Simpozij/Symposium.**
Edited by Janez Stanonik.   Ljubljana: Tiskala universitetna tiskarna,
1981. 409p.

The symposium took place in Ljubljana, 16-18 September 1981. The contributions
include a study of the impact of 'The native's return' by Ivan Cizmič, an analysis of
Adamič's radical pamphlet 'Struggle' by Henry H. Christian, and a study by the
distinguished ethnologist Marija Stanonik on the relationship between the American
writer and Yugoslav folklore. A celebration of Adamič as much as a scholarly
exercise, the papers are either in English or Slovene. For another appreciation of
Adamič, see John L. Modič, 'Laughing in the jungle: the writer as hero', *Slovene
Studies*, vol. 4, no. 2 (1982), p. 113-22.

88   **Captain John Smith in Slovenia.**
Janez Stanonik.   *Slovene Studies*, vol. 11, nos. 1-2 (1989), p. 25-32.

John Smith was one of the founders of Jamestown, the earliest permanent English
settlement in North America. Smith spent some time in Graz in the early seventeenth
century and Stanonik speculates as to the Slovene ethnic identity of some of the
villages he visited.

89   **A paper house: the ending of Yugoslavia.**
Mark Thompson.   London: Hutchinson Radius, 1992. 2nd ed. 322p.

Thompson was the London-based correspondent for *Mladina* when he wrote this
personal account of the twilight days of Yugoslavia. Chapter 1, 'Slovenian spring',
contains many witty recorded conversations with acquaintances and journalists,
together with a discussion of the 'highlights' of Slovenian national culture.

90 **Journal of a tour made in the years 1828-9 through Styria, Carniola, and Italy, whilst accompanying the late Sir Humphrey Davy.**
J. J. Tobin.   London: W. S. Orr, 1832. 242p.

A rambling and anecdotal account of one the last fishing trips made by Humphrey Davy, written by his companion. Tobin noted his dislike of Slovene cuisine, especially smoked pears, but enjoyed the fruits of their labour. At Bled, he recalled: 'the lake was beautifully tranquil and clear, and in the shade of the mountains, for the evening was already set in, resembled an extensive surface of black polished marble, only ruffled by the paddle of the canoe which bore us across it . . . we had part of the fish for supper' (p. 143).

Personal Memoirs

91 Yugoslav refugees in Italy: the story of a transit camp.
Anne Dacie, with a foreword by Compton Mackenzie.   London: Victor
Gollanz, 1945. 19p.

A collection of memoirs of the war years gathered among Yugoslavs displaced by the
fighting and living in Italy.

92 Balkan express.
Slavenka Drakulić.   London: Random House, 1993. 146p.

Writing between April 1991 and May 1992, the Croatian feminist describes her
reaction to the disintegration of Yugoslavia. Many of the pieces were written in the
relative safety of a flat in Ljubljana during the war in Croatia. In 'The smell of
independence' (p. 53-9), she writes about the absurdity of the borders that divide what
was once one country.

93 Twelve months with Tito's partisans.
William Jones.   Bedford, England: Bedford Books, 1946. 128p.

Vivid memoirs by a British officer fighting in Croatia and Slovenia, including rather
hagiographic portraits of Kardelj and Kidrič.

94 Struggle.
Edvard Kardelj, translated by Louis Adamič, with a preface by the
translator.   Los Angeles: A. Whipple, 1934. 41p.

Edvard Kardelj retells his own experiences as a Communist during a time when the
party was illegal and he faced imprisonment.

95 **Reminiscences: the struggle for recognition and independence: the new Yugoslavia, 1944-1957.**
Edvard Kardelj, translated by David Norris. London: Blond and Briggs in association with Summerfield, 1982. 279p.

Edvard Kardelj (1910-79) was arguably the second most important Yugoslavian Communist after Tito and the latter's right-hand man until he loyally died a year before the great man. In this book, based on interviews recorded shortly before his death, he recounts the highlights of his political career, including the partisan war and post-war reconstruction, the break with Cominform in 1948, and the development of Yugoslavian socialism, including self-management. In the immediate post-independence years, Kardelj, whose name once graced the University of Ljubljana, has been largely disregarded as the 'father' of the Slovenian nation, but perhaps history will judge this quiet former primary schoolteacher to be a figure of immense significance.

96 **Beacons in the night. With the OSS and Tito's partisans in wartime Yugoslavia.**
Frank Lindsay. Stanford, California: Stanford University Press, 1993. xxii, 383p. maps.

The memoirs of a retired American businessman. He recounts his wartime experiences alongside the Slovenian National Liberation Army in Styria from 1944 to 1945. One of the best and most historically accurate books on the war yet published. Some photographs are included.

97 **Peace and war: growing up in fascist Italy.**
Wanda Newby. London: Picador, 1992. 186p.

In this moving account of heroism in the face of overwhelming odds, the author recalls her childhood in the Karst, before her family's forcible exile to Parma in an attempt by the Mussolini government to break the backbone of the intelligentsia in the Slovene ethnic areas. During this time she helped her future husband Eric Newby to learn the Italian language, which facilitated his own escape.

98 **Guerrilla surgeon.**
Lindsay Rogers. London: Collins, 1957. 254p.

Presents the diary of a New Zealand surgeon who moved from service with a British medical unit behind the lines in wartime Yugoslavia to join the partisans in action on Viš, and through mainland Croatia, Bosnia and Slovenia: he later received Orders of Bravery and Merit from the Yugoslavians. His book records the action and role of a medic, as well as narrating the political transition from broad anti-fascism to communism amongst the partisans.

99 **The bale out.**
Edi Šelhaus. Ljubljana: Republiski odbor zveze zduzenj borcev NOV, 1976. 54p.

A story of courage and co-operation which recounts many successful attempts by the Communist partisans to rescue American prisoners-of-war and Allied pilots in the Slovene territories, which were then under German and Italian occupation. See also

Šelhaus's *Evasion and repatriation: Slovene partisans and rescued American airmen in World War II* (Manhattan, Kansas: Sunflower University Press, 1993. 233p.).

100 Between Hitler and Tito: Nazi occupation and Communist oppression.
Ljubo Sirc.   London: André Deutsch, 1989. 224p.

A moving autobiography and war reminiscences from one of Slovenia's leading dissidents of the Communist period. Extracts were also published sporadically in *South Slav Journal* from 1979 onwards.

Flora and Fauna

101   *Proteus anguinus* – the mysterious human fish.
Marko Aljančič, Boris Bulog, Arne Hodalič, Andrej Krancj, Peter
Skoberne.   Ljubljana: Vitrium, 1993. 80p.

The 'mysterious human fish' *Proteus anguinus* (a kind of blind albino amphibian)
lives in Karstic watercourses. In the nineteenth century it was caught by the Karst
peasants who sold it as a curiosity in Trieste. This superbly photographed study gives
a full description of the animal and discusses its historical and zoological significance.

102   **Carnian coral-sponge reefs in the Amphiclina beds between
Hudajužna and Zakriž (Western Slovenia).**
Stanko Buser, Bojan Ogorelec, Dragica Turnšek.   Ljubljana:
Slovenska akademija znanosti in umetnosti, 1982. 48p.

Investigates the lithological composition of the Amphiclina beds in the west of
Slovenia. Eighteen of the species are new, including one of the coral species.
According to their position, the reefs can be attributed to the Julian age. The text is in
English with a Slovene summary.

103   **Cave dwelling pseudoscorpions of the Dinaric Karst.**
Božidar P. M. Čurčič.   Ljubljana: Slovenska akademija znanosti in
umetnosti, 1988. 191p.

The lithological and ecological peculiarities of the Karst have engendered an unusual
and specialized flora and fauna. This study surveys the nature and distribution of the
group of small arachnids commonly referred to as 'pseudoscorpions'.

104 **Revision of the cave-dwelling and related species of the genus**
Troglohyphantes **Joseph (Linyphidae) with special reference to the**
Yugoslav species.
Christa L. Deeleman-Reinhold. Ljubljana: Slovenska akademija
znanosti in umetnosti, 1978. 219p. maps.

Describes the 54 forms of the spider genus *Troglohyphantes* in former Yugoslavia,
and their habitats. The work includes a map of cavernicole and microcavernicole
Troglohyphantes in Slovenia (p. 197). The text is in English with a Slovene summary,
and there is an extensive technical bibliography.

105 **Monography of the family Scutariellidae (Turbellana,**
Temnocephalidea).
Janez Matjašič. Ljubljana: Slovenska akademija znanosti in
umetnosti, 1990. 167p. maps.

A comprehensive survey of 22 species of temnocephalids of the Scutariellidae family,
16 of which are found in Europe. The study includes a distribution map of
Scutariellidae in Slovenia. Many of the Slovenian species live in and around the Karst
caves, but they are also found further south in the Dinaric Karst. The text is in
English, but includes a Slovene summary and black-and-white photographs, 29 plates
in all.

106 **Perspectives in microbial ecology.**
Edited by F. Megusar, M. Gantar. Ljubljana: Slovene Society for
Microbiology, 1986. 684p.

These are the edited Proceedings of the Fourth International Symposium on Microbial
Ecology, held Ljubljana in 1986.

107 *Allolobophora altimontana* **sp. n. (Oligochaeta lumbricidae) in**
certain associations in Slovenia.
Narcis Mršič. *Biološki vestnik*, vol 30, no. 2 (1982), p. 57-62.

A study of a new species of annelid worm found in Slovenia.

108 **Flowers in Slovenia.**
Luka Pintar, text by Tone Wraber, introduction by Matjaž Kmecl,
translated by Dejan Sušnik, Martin Cregeen. Ljubljana: Drzavna
založba Slovenije, 1990. 175p.

This beautifully photographed guide to the indigenous and more widespread plants
that grow in Slovenia includes a rather eccentric commentary. A detailed survey of the
flowers of the Karst area is also available; see Renato Mezzena, *Flora del Carso*
(Trieste: LINT, 1965. 355p.).

109 **The rudist fauna of Snežnik.**
Mario Pleničar. Ljubljana: Slovenska akademija znanosti in umetnosti, 1982. 26p. (Razprave, Dissertationes XX VI/I).

A richly illustrated guide – which includes 10 plates – to the fauna found within fossils around Mount Snežnik in southwestern Slovenia. The Sennonian biostroms consist almost entirely of rudist valves. The book describes seven genera, seven species (two of which were previously unknown to palaeontologists) and one entirely new subspecies.

110 **Flora carniolica.** (The flowers of Carniola.)
Giovanni Antonio Scopoli. Graz, Austria: Akademischer Druck und Verlagsanstalt, 1972. 2 vols.

Originally published in 1772, this comprehensive guide to the flora of Carniola (the Habsburg province of Krain, or Kranjska in Slovene) by an naturalist who specialized in the ecology of the Eastern Alps is complemented by a reprint of Scopoli's other main work on Carniolan nature *Entomologia carniolica* (The insects of Carniola) (Graz: Akademischer Druck und Verlagsanstalt, 1972. 418p.).

111 **The miracle of propolis.**
Mitja Vosnjak. Wellingborough, England: Thorsons, 1978. 93p.

As a nation, the Slovenes are quite enamoured by alternative medicine from herbal teas to cabbage compresses as a putative cure for arthritis. Propolis ('the Slovenian ginseng'), the resinous matter collected from buds by bees and used to build their hives, was first investigated by Anton Janša (1734-73), an expert beekeeper. It was argued by another Slovene, Rado Seifert, that the substance has antibiotic properties which are discussed in the current book. Thanks to Seifert and Janša, it is now possible to buy propolis as a food supplement in health food stores. This book was originally issued as *Propolis, zdravilo jutrišnega dne* (Propolis, the medicine of yesteryear) (Ljubljana: Mladinska knjiga, 1977. 135p.).

Prehistory and Archaeology

112 **Human skeletal remains in Slovenia.**
J. L. Angel. In: *Mecklenburg Collection, Part 1.* Edited by Hugh
Hencken. Cambridge, Massachusetts: Peabody Museum, Harvard
University, 1968, p. 73-108. (*American School of Prehistoric Research
Bulletin*, no. 25).
A survey of existing knowledge about skeletal remains in the Slovene lands, this
volume also includes an article by the editor on the Iron Age cemetery of
Magdalenska gora.

113 **50 years of Paleolithic research in Slovenia.**
Mitja Brodar. *Arheološki vestnik*, vol. 30 (1979), p. 21-8.
A survey of the work of Slovenian archaeologists on Stone Age sites.

114 **The Iron Age cemetery of Magdalenska gora in Slovenia.**
Hugh Hencken. Cambridge, Massachusetts: Peabody Museum,
Harvard University, 1978. 361p. (*American School of Prehistoric
Research Bulletin*, no. 32).
An extended field report of material excavated from the Hallstadt period. See also,
'The world of the Magdalenska gora', by Peter S. Wells, *Harvard Magazine*, vol. 80,
no. 6 (July/Aug. 1978), p. 36-41.

115 **Umetnost Situla / Situla art.**
Jože Kastelič, with contributions by Karl Kromer and Guido
Mansuelli, photographs by Mladen Grčević. Belgrade: Jugoslavija
Publishers, 1956. 80p. map.
Reviews the Situla art in Slovenia, particularly the Hallstadt Situla from the sixth
century, which was excavated in Vače in 1882.

Prehistory and Archaeology

116   **Pismo brez pisave: arheologija o prvih stoletjih krščanstva na Slovenskem / Letter without written word: the archaeology of the first centuries of Christianity in Slovenia.**
Timotej Knifič, Milan Šagadin, translated by Philip F. J. Mason.
Ljubljana: Narodni muzej, 1991. 132p.

Survey of extant material concerning the initial establishment of Christianity in the Slovene lands, which includes an illustrated catalogue of 122 items from this period. It includes facsimiles and both English and Slovene text. Of related interest in the same series is *Modularna evritmija šempeterskih edikul/The modular eurythmyia of aediculae in Šempeter*, by T. Kurent (Ljubljana: Narodni muzej, 1970. 100p.).

117   **The castle hill of Ptuj from prehistoric times to the Middle Ages.**
J. Korošec. *Archaeology*, vol. 8, no. 3 (Sept. 1955), p. 162-8.

Ptuj in Slovenian Styria has been settled from the earliest times. Known to the Romans as Poetovio and during the Habsburg period as Pettau, it most imposing feature is its castle, which has been restored to its full glory since the Second World War. Here, Jože Korošec, one of the leading authorities on the history of this area, discusses the castle site before the present castle was constructed in the sixteenth century. See also his *Poročilo o izkopavanju na ptujskem gradu, leta 1946/Report on the archaeological excavations on the castle hill of Ptuj in 1946* (Ljubljana: Slovenska akademija znanosti in umetnosti, 1947. 61p.). The text is in English and Slovene.

118   **The monetary circulation in the southeastern Alpine region, ca. 300 B.C. – A.D. 1000.**
Ljubljana: Narodni muzej, 1986. 263p. maps. (Series: Situla 24).

A discussion of the development of a money economy in the wider eastern Alp region. The book also contains 10 plates of photographs of the coins in the collection of the National Museum. The text is in English and Slovene.

119   **Severno emonsko grobišče / The northern necropolis of Emona.**
Ljudmila Plesničar-Gec.   Ljubljana: Narodni muzej, 1972. 272p.

Emona was the Roman name for the Ljubljana city site. This book presents a complete illustrated catalogue of the items that were found during excavations of the graveyards, with a commentary in English and Slovene. It contains 225 plates. On Ancient Emona, see also: Tine Kurent and Milica Detoni, *Modularna rekonstrucija Emone/The modular reconstruction of Emona* (Ljubljana: Narodni muzej, 1963. 71p.). The text is again in English and Slovene.

120   **Starokrščanski center v Emoni / Old Christian center in Emona.**
Ljudmila Plesničar-Gec in collaboration with Jaroslav Šašel, Irena Sivec, Iva Mikl-Curk, Peter Kos.   Ljubljana: Tisk mestnega muzeja, 1983. 151p. maps.

The staff of the town museum have produced a richly illustrated guide to the excavation work undertaken after 1955 on the Emona (Ljubljana) site. It includes 63 plates and a complete catalogue of the finds. The mosaics described by Jaroslav Šašel (p. 57-9) probably date back to the later half of the fourth century AD when Christianity became firmly rooted in this region.

30

121 **Kranj-Krizišče Iskra / Kranj-Iskra crossroads.**
Milan Sagadin. Ljubljana: Narodni muzej, Tiskana Jože Moskrič, 1987. 158p.

This book catalogues 279 early medieval and 264 later skeletons that were found on an excavated gravel terrace on the banks of the river Sava in Kranj in 1977, near to the Iskra factory. These finds date from the earliest Slavonic period. The text is in English and Slovene, and there are 65 plates and 19 appendices.

122 **The excavations of Stična in Slovenia by the Duchess of Mecklenburg, 1905-1914.**
Peter S. Wells. *Journal of Field Archaeology*, vol. 5, no. 2 (1978), p. 215-26.

Wells discusses the fieldwork written by Marie, Duchess of Mecklenburg-Schwerin. The original appeared as *Prehistoric grave material from Carniola excavated in 1905-14* (New York: American Art Association, Anderson Galleries, 1934. 131p. maps.).

123 **The emergence of an Iron Age economy: the Mecklenburg grave groups from Hallstadt and Stična.**
Peter S. Wells. Cambridge, Massachusetts: Peabody Museum, Harvard University, 1981. 206p. (*American School of Prehistoric Research Bulletin*, no. 33).

Compares the Iron Age finds of Stična with those from the 'classic' Hallstadt site in Germany. Wells includes extensive field notes and illustrations.

124 **Socio-economic aspects of the amber trade in early Iron Age Slovenia.**
Peter S. Wells. *Journal of Baltic Studies*, vol. 16, no. 3 (Fall 1985), p. 268-75.

Reviews the evidence for the importation of amber from northern Europe to the southeastern Alpine region. The principal centres in present-day Slovenia were at Stična, Magdalenska gora, Vače and Novo mesto, which were probably focal points of a tribal group or chiefdom. The quantity of amber in graves at Stična varies between one and 159 beads, which leads Wells to discuss the anthropological function of amber in these societies.

125 **Ostrogothic coinage from collections in Croatia, Slovenia and Bosnia and Hercegovina.**
Demo Željko. Ljubljana: Narodni muzej, 1994. xv, 323p.

A catalogue of excavated coins from the the pre-Slavonic period in the northern part of the former Yugoslavia.

History

The general area

126   The making of the Habsburg monarchy 1550-1700, an interpretation.
R. J. W. Evans.   Oxford: Clarendon Press, 1979. Reprinted William Clowes: London, 1984. 531p. maps.

The standard history of the early modern Habsburg monarchy, which includes reference to material about the Slovene lands and their historiography.

127   Crown, Church and Estates. Central European politics in the sixteenth and seventeenth centuries.
Edited by R. J. W. Evans, T. V. Thomas.   London: Macmillan, in association with the School of Slavonic and East European Studies, University of London, 1991. 321p.

A region-by-region study of the workings of the Habsburg polity which includes a case-study of Inner Austria, the administrative unit which covered modern-day Slovenia. 'Crowns, Estates amd the financing of defence in Inner Austria 1500-1630', by the eminent Slovene historian Sergei Vilfan (p. 70-9), deals with the connections between financial developments, the Reformation and military history. The collection as a whole is important, in that this is an area which has hitherto been neglected in English-language scholarship.

128   History of the Balkans.
Barbara Jelavich.   Cambridge: Cambridge University Press, 1983. 2 vols. maps.

One of the finest histories of the area, which includes an analysis of the rise of Slovenian national consciousness.

129   **The peoples of the Eastern Habsburg lands, 1526-1918.**
Robert A. Kann, Zdenek V. David.   Seattle: University of Washington
Press, 1984. 543p. maps.
One of the most comprehensive treatments of Slovene history within a general
historical volume, the narrative being divided both by national group and by period.
A highly recommended account.

130   **A history of mediaeval Austria.**
Allen W. A. Leeper, edited posthumously by R. W. Seton-Watson,
C. A. Macartney.   Oxford: Oxford University Press, 1941. 420p.
This book gives a survey of the early history of the Slovene territories of Carniola,
Carinthia, Styria and the Adriatic coast, from the settlement of the area to the
thirteenth century. Although the author was acquainted with individual national
histories of the area, the approach he adopted was synthetic rather than ethnocentric
and as such, this is a useful foil to other medieval histories.

131   **The Habsburg Empire 1790-1918.**
C. A. Macartney.   London: Weidenfeld & Nicholson, 1971. 908p.
maps.
A classic narrative account of the final years of the Habsburg monarchy by a
distinguished British historian.

132   **A short history of the Yugoslav peoples.**
Fred Singleton.   Cambridge: Cambridge University Press, 1985.
Reprinted 1993. 309p.
A comprehensive and scholarly survey of 'Yugoslav' history that treats each
nationality separately within an integrated chronological format.

Slovenia

133   **Zgodovina Slovencev.** (A history of the Slovenes.)
Editor-in-chief Zdenko Čepič.   Ljubljana: Cankarjeva založba, 1979.
964p.
This monumental work was written by Slovenia's finest historians, including Ferdo
Gestrin, Bogo Grafenauer, Metod Mikuž, and Vasilij Melik.

134   **Geschichte Krains bis auf das Jahr 1813.** (A history of Carniola to
1813.)
August Dimitz.   Ljubljana/Laibach: Druck und Verlag Ig von
Kleinmayr und Fed. Bamberg, 1874-76. 4 vols.
The standard comprehensive history of the pre-nineteenth-century period.

135   **The Slovenes from the earliest times: illustrated story of Slovenia.**
Draga Gelt.   Victoria: Co-ordinating Committee of Slovenian
Organisations in Victoria, Australia, 1985. 210p.

An illustrated narrative history of Slovenia intended for the children of Slovenes who
settled in Australia.

136   **The Slovenes: a social history from the earliest times to 1910.**
Dragotin Lončar, translated by Antony J. Klančar.   Cleveland, Ohio:
American Jugoslav Printing and Publishers, 1939. 77p.

A history of the Slovenes, designed for the children of those who emigrated to the
United States and Canada before the Second World War.

137   **A brief history of Slovenia: historical background of the Republic
of Slovenia.**
Janko Prunk, Wayne Tuttle, Majda Klander.   Ljubljana: Založba
Mihelač, 1994. 85p.

This elementary history of Slovenia is an ideal starting place for the tourist or visitor
with a little time to spare.

138   **Rechtsgeschichte der Slowenen bis zum Jahre 1941.** (A legal history
of the Slovenes to 1941.)
Sergei Vilfan.   Graz, Austria: Leykam, 1968. 242p.

A history of the Slovenes and the legal institutions of the Habsburg period and royalist
Yugoslavia, written by an acknowledged international expert.

139   **A bulwark against Germany: the fight of the Slovenes, the western
branch of the Yugoslavs for national existence.**
Bogumil Vošnjak, translated by Fanny S. Copeland.   London: Allen
and Unwin, 1917. 270p. map.

Written during the First World War, this book is notable for its anti-German
sentiments in that it narrates Slovene history as a heroic ethnic struggle of one group
against another. See also Vošnjak's *A dying empire: Central Europe, Pan-Germanism
and the downfall of Austria–Hungary* (London: G. Allen and Unwin, 1918. 198p.
map).

140   **A chapter of the old Slovene democracy.**
Bogumil Vošnjak.   London: Murray, 1917. 24p.

Bogumil Vošnjak was an extraordinary writer and promoter of the Slovenian national
cause, joint author of the Corfu Declaration (see *South Slav Journal*, vol. 9, nos. 3-4
(1986), p. 25), professor of Law at Ljubljana University and Yugoslavian diplomat.
Here, in his capacity as promoter, he discusses the medieval origins of 'Slovene
democracy' within the investiture in Carinthia.

To 1500

141 Aspects of the Slavic Middle Ages and Slavic Renaissance culture.
Henrik Birnbaum. New York: Peter Lang Publishers, 1991. [n.p.].
(American University Studies, Series XII, Slavic Languages and
Literature, vol. 4).

Chapter one, entitled 'Slavic migration routes into Southeastern Europe and early
divisions of the Southern Slavs' (p. 1-24), examines the early movement of Slavonic
tribes into Southeastern Europe. Birnbaum looks in particular at the early relationship
between the Croatian Kajkavian dialect and Slovene.

142 'Caranthani Marahenses' and 'Moravi sive Karinthi'.
Imre Boba. *Slovene Studies*, vol. 4, no. 2 (1982), p. 83-90.

The links between the various Slavonic tribes, before the division into distinct 'ethnic'
groups is a contentious historical topic. Boba here discusses the link between
'Moravian' and 'Carinthian' culture in the early Middle Ages. Using the combined
evidence of the writings of Cosmos and Helmold and the Frankish annals, he
concludes that the Moravians of Moimar, Ratislav and Sventopolk had direct and
close contacts with Caranthania (the forerunner of Carinthia) throughout their political
existence. He also concludes that, at least from AD 874, Moravia proper with a centre
in Morava on the river Sava was intermittently subordinated to the Marchgraves of
Carinthia. This connection therefore helps to explain the presence of South Slavic,
especially Alpine artefacts amongst the archaeological finds in Bohemia and Moravia.

143 Slovene mediaeval history: selected studies.
Aloysius L. Kuhar. New York; Washington, DC: Studia Slovenica,
1962. 143p.

A series of articles on some of the more salient problems of Slovene medieval history,
which include a discussion of the contents of the Freising fragments (the earliest
known Slavonic manuscript), the work of Irish missionaries, the installation of the
Dukes of Karantanija, and the remnants of Glagolitic scripts in the Slovene lands.
Published posthumously, the appendices were prepared by Hrvoj Maister.

**144 The conversion of the Slovenes and the German–Slav ethnic
boundary in the Eastern Alps.**
Aloysius L. Kuhar. New York; Washington, DC: Studia Slovenica,
1967. 231p.

Although written at times from a rather epic 'ethnic' angle, the book provides an
almost parish-by-parish account of the spread of Christianity across the Slovene lands
from the sixth century onwards, beginning from the missionary bases in Bavaria,
Aquileia and Pannonia. A very fine piece of historical scholarship, presented in a clear
and accessible manner.

1500-1918

145 **Economie et société en Slovènie au XVIe siècle.** (Economy and society in Slovenia in the sixteenth century.)
Ferdo Gestrin. *Annales: Economies, Sociétés, Civilisations*, vol. 17, no. 4 (July-Aug. 1962), p. 663-90.

A detailed survey of the trade in the Slovene lands in the sixteenth century, concentrating in particular on the Idrija mercury mines and the coastal trade. See also Gestrin's *Land occupation, settlement and frontiers of Slovenia from the 16th to the beginning of the 20th century* (Ljubljana: Mladinska knjiga, 1962. 62p.).

146 **A comparison of economic and social conditions in Slovene and Croatian lands during the Reformation.**
Toussaint Hočevar. *Slovene Studies*, vol. 8, nos. 1-2 (1984), p. 31-48.

Hočevar argues that Slovenia was more economically developed than Croatia in the sixteenth century, particularly in terms of urban development, and was therefore more receptive to Reformation ideas.

147 **Humanism in the Slovene lands.**
Rado L. Lenček. *Nationalities Papers*, vol. 7, no. 2 (Fall 1979), p. 155-70.

Discusses the 'Slovene Humanism period' from approximately 1450 to 1525. The appendix to the article includes a bibliographical summary of the major humanists active in the Slovene lands. The most authoratative full-length study of this subject is *Humanizem na Slovenskem* (Humanism in the Slovene lands) by Primož Simoniti (Ljubljana: Slovenska matica, 1979).

148 **The controversy about the Kosezi in Slovene historiography.**
Bogdan C. Novak. *Slovene Studies*, vol. 4, no. 2 (1982), p. 127-53.

The *Kosezi* or *Edlinge* were a group of serfs in sixteenth-century Slovenia, but with special privileges and special duties to perform. Both the Croat Ljudomil Hauptman and the Slovene Josip Mal had theories about the origins of this group, which Novak contrasts with the later theories of Bogo Grafenauer and Milko Kos.

149 **The rise of modern Slovenian historiography.**
Michael. B. Petrovich. *Journal of Central European Affairs*, vol. 22, no. 4 (1963), p. 440-67.

'Slovenia' did not exist either as a geographical concept or as a political reality before the eighteenth century. By examining the work of six early modern historians who were either of Slovene ethnic origin or living in the Slovene lands of the Habsburg monarchy, Petrovich traces the evolution of provincial – and therefore largely territorial – loyalties to national loyalties and notions of 'Slovene' ethnos. Early historians, such as Christalnick (d. 1595), Schoenleben (1618-81), Valvasor (1641-93) and Thalnitscher (1655-1719) had a strong sense of regional identity, whereas romantic nationalism is more evident in the work of Pohlin (1735-1801) and Linhart (1756-95).

150 **Hexenprozesse in Slowenien.** (Witchcraft trials in Slovenia.)
Vincenc Rajšp. *Acta Etnografica* (Budapest), vol. 37, nos. 1-4
(1991/2), p. 51-66.

An examination of the withcraft trials in Slovenia, particularly in the late seventeenth and early eighteenth century.

151 **Korespondenca Janeza Vajkarda Valvasorja z Royal Society/The correspondence of Janez Vajkard Valvasor with the Royal Society.**
Branko Reisp, translated from Latin by Primož Simoniti, translated
into English by Alenka Goričan. Ljubljana: Slovenska akademija
znanosti in umetnosti, 1987. 113p.

A translation and catalogue of the correspondence between Valvasor, the Carniolan polymath and the Royal Society in London, between 1685 and 1688. The introduction and commentaries are translated into English, although the original letters in Latin have been translated only into Slovene.

152 **The Slovene and Yugoslavism, 1890-1914.**
Carole Rogel. Boulder, Colorado: East European Quarterly; New
York: Columbia University Press, 1977. 167p. bibliog. (East European
Monographs, no. 24).

During the nineteenth century, Slovenian nationalism grew in a similar way to other Central European nationalisms, with cultural nationalism preceding political demands. This book is a study of the last years of the Habsburg monarchy in the context of growing Slovenian Yugoslavism, particularly among the *preporodovci*, or radical students. As it has become fashionable to emphasize the Slovenes' reluctance to become part of a Yugoslavian state in recent years, this study is a useful counter-balance, emphasizing the importance of Yugoslavism for the growth of national consciousness. For earlier versions of the above monographs see also two articles by Carole Rogel: 'The Slovenes and political Yugoslavism on the eve of World War I', *East European Quarterly*, vol. 4, no. 4 (1971), p. 408-18; and 'Preporodovci: Slovene students for an independent Yugoslavia', *Canadian Slavic Studies*, vol. 5, no. 1 (1968), p. 46-67.

153 **The Slovenes in the revolutionary period.**
Carole Rogel. In: *Consortium on Revolutionary Europe*: Proceedings,
Tallahassee, Florida, Vol. I (1980), p. 264-74.

Assesses the impact of French rule and French ideas on Slovenian national consciousness.

154 **Slovene and Croatian land in the sixteenth century (a geographical framework).**
Jože Velikonja. *Slovene Studies*, vol. 6, nos. 1-2 (1984), p. 11-30.

A clearly illustrated survey of the Slovene and Croat lands, discussing trade links in particular. It is beautifully accompanied by contemporary maps.

155 **The Slovenes and the Habsburg monarchy.**
Fran Zwitter. *Austrian History Yearbook*, vol. 3, no. 2 (1967), p. 159-88.

Looks at Slovene political development from the early cultural nationalism of the early nineteenth century through to the Yugoslavism of the immediate pre-First World War period. See also 'Illyrisme et le sentiment yougoslave', *Le Monde Slave* (April 1933), p. 39-71; (May 1933), p. 161-85; and (June 1933), p. 358-75. Of related interest is Fran Zwitter, in collaboration with Jaroslav Šidak and Vašo Bogdanov, *Les problèmes nationaux dans la monarchie des Habsbourg* (National problems in the Habsburg monarchy) (Belgrade: Comité National Yougoslave des Sciences Historiques, 1960. 148p.).

1918 onwards

156 **The interests of the Third Reich in Slovenia.**
Tone Ferenc. In: *The Third Reich and Yugoslavia 1933-45*. Edited by Života Anić, Pero Morača. Belgrade: Institut za savremenu istoriju, 1977, p. 502-16.

The proceedings of a conference, *Treči Rajh i Jugoslavija 1933-1945*, held in Belgrade in October 1973, which was organized by the Institute for Contemporary History and the Institute for the Recent History of Nations and Nationalism (Zajednica Institucija za noviju istoriju naroda i narodnosti) in Belgrade. The texts are mainly in English, with an introduction in Serbo-Croat. For a contemporary account, see: Elizabeth Wiskeman, 'The Drang nach Osten continues', *Foreign Affairs*, vol. 17, no. 4 (July 1939), p. 764-73, which discusses the German attempts to woo the Slovenes away from the 'primitive' Serbs.

157 **The martyrdom of the Slovenes.**
Lillian F. Gray. *Contemporary Review*, no. 926 (Feb. 1943), p. 108-13.

Tells of the atrocities committed by the Axis powers during the Second World War in Slovenia. For a similar account, see: John La Farge, *The martyrdom of Slovenia* (New York: American Press, 1942. 24p.), as well as Boris Furlan, *Fighting Yugoslavia – the struggle of the Slovenes* (New York: Yugoslav Information Service, 1942. 38p.).

158 **Slovenia under Nazi occupation, 1941-45.**
Helga H. Harriman. New York: Studia Slovenica, 1977. 94p. maps. bibliog.

The Nazis generally regarded the portion of Slovene Styria which they occupied from 1941 to 1945 to be part of greater Germany, although Harriman argues that national consciousness amongst this community was far more tenuous than was initially supposed by the German leadership and that they faced almost continuous resistance from 'disloyal' Slovenes. This short monograph is a good introduction in English to this terrible and brutal period. See also Harriman's 'Slovenia as an outpost of the Third Reich', *East European Quarterly*, vol. 5, no. 2 (June 1971), p. 222-31.

159 **Limits to Germandom: resistance to the Nazi annexation of Slovenia.**
Tim Kirk. *Slavonic and East European Review*, vol. 69, no. 4 (Oct. 1991), p. 646-67.

Kirk argues that ethnic Slovenes living in those parts of former Royalist Yugoslavia that had been annexed by the Nazis in 1941 (namely Southern Styria and parts of Carniola), represented the most serious guerrilla opposition to the policy of Germanization within the Third Reich. The author finds evidence of passive resistance and partisan activity amongst the Slovenes from 1941 and examines the regime's attempts to quell resistance by importing ethnic Germans to work in the area and by deporting Slovenes to the so-called Altreich (the pre-1938 Reich). There was also industrial unrest from those Slovene workers who opposed the regime. The successful partisan campaign and the collapse of Nazi power from 1944 onwards is then documented.

160 **Slovenia: an area of strain.**
Arthur E. Moodie. *Journal of Central European Affairs*, vol. 3, no. 1 (April 1943), p. 65-80.

Moodie reviews the geo-political position of the Slovene lands both before and up to 1943.

161 **War and revolution in Yugoslavia 1941-1945.**
Edited by Novak Strugar, Branko Prnjat. Belgrade: Aktuelna pitanja socijalizma, 1985. 284p.

This book of essays, published within the Socialist Thought and Practice series, includes 'The liberation of Istria, Trieste and the Slovenian littoral' by Uroš Kostić (p. 214-44), and a polemic entitled 'The National Question' by a Slovene authority Janko Pleterski (p. 61-87).

162 **Slovene losses 1941-1945.**
Peter Urbanc. *South Slav Journal*, vol. 11, no. 2-3 (Summer/Autumn 1988), p. 34-9.

Edvard Kardelj issued a figure of 1,700,000 casualties of the Second World War in Yugoslavia, although according to later estimates the numbers killed were probably about 1 million. Milovan Djilas estimated that only about 10 per cent of those killed were murdered by the occupying forces, the others by fellow Yugoslavs. This article considers in detail those Slovenes who were killed and by whom. See also John Prčela, 'Massacre sites in Slovenia', in *Operation Slaughterhouse; eyewitness accounts of postwar massacres in Yugoslavia*. Edited by John Prčela and Stanko Guldescu (Philadelphia: Dorrance, 1970, p. 353-93).

163 **The Klagenfurt conspiracy: the forcible repartriation of Yugoslav royalists.**
Staniša Vlahović. *South Slav Journal*, vol. 11, no. 2-3 (Summer-Autumn 1988), p. 28-34.

Discusses the Klagenfurt conspiracy, or what Vlahović calls 'Tito's Katyn', introducing new documentation from the Public Record Office in London, which he argues casts new light on the shameful story behind the forcible repatriation of Royalists to Slovenia after the war.

164   **The Slovenes and Yugoslavia.**
    Peter Vodopivec.   *East European Politics and Society*, vol. 6, no. 3 (Fall 1992), p. 220-41.

Even before the First World War and the collapse of the Habsburg monarchy, as Vodopivec states, the Slovenes were aware that the creation of a Yugoslavian state dominated by Belgrade centralism could create a 'Piedmont' problem (i.e., the dominance of one province over the rest). Leading Slovenes, including Ivan Cankar, felt that a looser federation along Swiss lines was a more suitable solution for the region, given the different traditions of the South Slav peoples. Slovenian autonomism and the survival of cultural stereotypes about the Serbs (and vice versa) plagued both Royalist and Communist Yugoslavia, surfacing in such issues as the fall of the Slovenian communist chief Stane Kavčič in 1972. Vodopivec argues that these autonomist strains finally broke the Yugoslavian federation in the late 1980s, when Slovenian political expression moved from 'Herder to Hegel'. On the Yugoslav period see also: Rudolph M. Šušel, 'The Slovenes and Yugoslavia, 1918-1929' (PhD dissertation, Indiana University, 1973. 347p.).

Population, Nationalities and Minorities

The National Question

165 **The National Question in Yugoslavia: origins, history, politics.**
Ivo Banac. Ithaca, New York: Cornell University Press, 1984. 452p.
maps.

This extremely authoritative history of the whole of the former Yugoslavia considers the Slovenes separately.

166 **Class and nation in Slovenia. Edvard Kardelj versus Josip Vidmar.**
Kenneth E. Basom. *East European Quarterly*, vol. 26, no. 2
(Summer 1992), p. 209-18.

In 1932, Josip Vidmar, a left-wing intellectual published a study *Kulturni problem Slovenstva* (The cultural problem of the Slovenes), in which he argued that the Slovene language was a crucial cultural artefact, which should be preserved. The book was banned by King Alexander's royal dictatorship for its lack of 'Yugoslav loyalty'. The Slovene marxist Edvard Kardelj criticized the book for its 'petty bourgeois character'. According to Basom, Kardelj held that nations would be superseded by an international economic order, which would generate a new world culture. Kardelj thus rejected Vidmar's permanent association of the nation with culture (p. 214). He later developed his criticism into a more serious corpus of work, culminating in *Razvoj slovenskega narodnega vprašanja* (The development of the Slovene National Question) (Ljubljana: Naša založba, 1939) under the pseudonym of Sperans.

167 **Slovenians meet Woodrow Wilson.**
Vlado Bevc. *South Slav Journal*, vol. 11, no. 2-3 (Summer/Autumn
1988), p. 18-24.

At the Paris Peace Conference of 1919, the Slovene section of the Yugoslav delegation, Drs Vošnjak, Gregorin and Svegel met the American President Woodrow Wilson to discuss the status of Slovene ethnic territory. A report of an audience with Wilson was recorded by Ivan Svegel on 26 April 1919, and is reproduced here in full.

168 **Austro-Slavism as the motive of Kopitar's work.**
Sergio Bonazza. *Slovene Studies*, vol. 5, no. 2 (1983), p. 155-64.
Bonazza argues that the linguist and court librarian Jernej Kopitar should be seen as 'the true founder of Austro-Slavism' (p. 163), in that he believed that the future for the Slavs lay with the Austrian rather than the Russian monarchy. He based his belief, in part, on the premise that Old Church Slavonic 'owed its beginnings to Cyril and Methodius in Pannonia, therefore to Austrian soil' (p. 156). Kopitar even planned to travel to Mount Athos himself to recover codices found there, but his plans came to nothing. The discovery of a Glagolitic script in Church Slavonic codex in the Tyrol in 1829 gave another boost to Kopitar's ideas in that 'in his cultural policies, Kopitar made use of the Catholic Church to the same extent that Russian Pan-Slavism utilised the Orthodox Church' (p. 159) Even his sponsorship of the great Serb poet Vuk Karadžić was in part motivated by a fear that the Serbs, if treated badly, might become even closer to the Russians.

169 **The third partner in Yugoslavia (Slovenia).**
Annie Christitch. *Contemporary Review*, no. 750 (June 1928), p. 19-31.
Slovenia's position in royalist Yugoslavia was as a 'partner' nation to the Croats and Serbs. However, after the proclamation of the Vidovdan constitution, the state was more clearly centralized in Belgrade.

170 **The Slovenes want to live.**
Joseph Clissold. London: Jugoslav Information Centre, 1943. 48p. map.
A plea for Slovenian territorial integrity during the middle of the Second World War, when Slovenia was partitioned between the Third Reich and Italy.

171 **The last years of Austria Hungary.**
Edited by Mark Cornwall. Exeter, England: University of Exeter Press, 1990. 155p. (Studies in History, no. 27).
A study of the twilight years of the great Imperial dynasty which, in part, draws its strength from the regional perspective that the different essays focus on. 'The Southern Slav question 1908-18' by Janko Pleterski (p. 77-100) provides a useful overview of these last years from one of Slovenia's foremost historians, which draws on previously unpublished material in the archives in Ljubljana. According to the Austrian Minister of the Interior, Heinold, in September 1914, the authorities in Styria 'already seem to see in every person of Slovene nationality a politically unreliable person' (p. 88). See also Janko Pleterski, 'The Slovenes', in *Habsburgermonarchie 1848-1918*, vol. 3, no. 2 (1980), p. 801-38. More recently the Austrian Slovene scholar Felix J. Bišter has produced a history of the political work of Anton Korošec before 1918 entitled, *Majestaet, es ist zu spaet . . . Anton Korošec und die slowenische Politik im Wiener Reichsrat bis 1918* (Majesty it is too late . . . Anton Korošec and Slovene political discourse in the Viennese Parliament to 1918) (Wien/Koeln/Weimar: Boehlau Verlag, 1995. 393p.).

172 **Mountain photography and the constitution of national identity.**
Ales Erjavec. *Filozofski vestnik*, vol. 15, no. 2 (1994), p. 211-34.

The author argues that mountain photography helped to constitute national identity in the Slovene lands in the nineteenth century, particularly with regard to the construction of Triglav as a national symbol.

173 **On the National Question.**
Edvard Kardelj. *Yugoslav Survey*, vol. 22, no. 4 (Nov. 1981), p. 3-30.

Kardelj's views on the relationship between socialism and nation are clearly set out here. For a commentary, see Carole Rogel, 'Edvard Kardelj's nationality theory and Yugoslav socialism', *Canadian Review of Studies in Nationalism*, vol. 12 (1985), p. 343-57.

174 **At the roots of Slovene intellectual disassociation from the Illyrian movement.**
Rado L. Lenček. *Slovene Studies*, vol. 4, no. 1 (1982), p. 41-8.

An extended review of Anton Linhart's *Versuch einer Geschichte von Krain und den uebrigen Laendern der suedlichen Slaven Oesterreichs* (An attempt at a history of Carniola and the other lands of the South Slavs of Austria), published in Ljubljana/ Laibach by W. H. Korn between 1788 and 1791. A Slovene translation of the German original appeared in 1981. Traditionally this text has been seen as 'one of the most significant fountain heads of the concept of the modern Slovene nation' (p. 41). Linhart rejected the idea of an Illyrian identity, stating that the Skipatar (Albanians) were Illyrian, but not Slavic. Lenček feels that Linhart's stance must have influenced those of his generation who did not participate in the Illyrian movement.

175 **A paradigm of Slavic national evolution: Bible, grammar, poet.**
Rado L. Lenček. *Slovene Studies*, vol. 8, nos. 1-2 (1984), p. 57-71.

Discusses the importance of the codification of the Slovene language for the process of national self-awareness.

176 **At the roots of Slovene national individuality.**
Bogdan C. Novak. *Papers in Slovene Studies*, vol. I (1975), p. 79-125.

By writing a narrative of notable events in the history of the Slovenes, from the tribal state of Carantania to political activities immediately before the First World War, the author sought to explain how the Slovenes came to be a distinctive nation. Novak feels that 'with the Enlightenment a Slovene national awakening really began' and devotes most of the article to the activities of intellectuals in the late eighteenth and nineteenth centuries. His definition of Slovene nationality is based on a linguistic rather than a regional concept. This essay represents a good introduction to a traditional history of the Slovenes and his footnotes guide the reader through the more specialized literature. Of related interest is S. W. Gould, 'The Slovenes: education and historical development versus national consciousness today', *Social Studies*, vol. 36 (1945), p. 310-15.

177 **Symbols, slogans and identity in the Slovene search for sovereignty 1987-91.**
Joseph Paternost. *Slovene Studies*, vol. 14, no. 1 (1992), p. 51-68.
Paternost examines some of the signifiers of Slovenian national identity: 'Triglav', 'lipa' (linden tree), 'Alpe' (the Alps), the idea that Slovenia is part of Europe and the notion that it was the most Western, the most developed and the most democratic of the Yugoslav republics' (p. 55).

178 **Development of the Slovene National Question.**
Anton Vratuša. *Socialist Thought and Practice*, vol. 28, no. 2 (March/April 1988), p. 84-95.
A discussion of Slovenian national development by a leading commentator of Yugoslavian affairs.

179 **Eastern Europe's republics of Gilead.**
Slavoj Žižek. *New Left Review*, vol. 30, no. 183 (Sept./Oct. 1990), p. 50-62.
Using Lacanian psychoanalysis to deconstruct elements of nationalist discourse in Eastern Europe, Žižek argues that national identification is a way in which an ethnic community organizes its enjoyment, and other ethnic groups are identified by their desire to ruin a putative way of life. To put this in psychoanalytic terms: the 'Nation-thing' is possessed and 'others' threaten to 'steal our enjoyment'. Thus in the former Yugoslavia every ethnic group 'built its own mythology narrating how other nations deprived it of the vital part of enjoyment the possession of which would allow it to live fully'. Slovenes saw Serbians and Bosnians as 'lazy', 'corrupt' and 'noisy', whereas Serbs criticized Slovenes for their 'unnatural dilligence, stiffness and selfish calculation'. Both stereotypes, argues Žižek, represent hatred of one's own enjoyment and paranoia. The call for 'national reconciliation' in Slovenia is the arena of what Žižek calls a 'crucial hegemonic struggle', as it is clear that this phrase means something rather different to advocates of Slovene essential unity than to those who reject the irreducibility of a 'multitude of dreams' to a national or ethnic identity.

National minorities

180 **L'identità etnica quale tipo di identità sociale: il caso degli Italiani di Jugoslavia.** (Ethnic identity as a type of social identity: the case of the Italian population of Yugoslavia.)
Loredana Bogiulin-Debeljuh. PhD dissertation, University of Ljubljana, 1991. 317p.
Outlines the ethnic and social position of Yugoslavia's Italian population, which is mainly found on the Slovenian and Croatian littoral.

181　**The Alpe-Adria as a multinational region.**
　　Silvo Devetak.　*Slovene Studies*, vol. 10, no. 1 (1988), p. 27-35.
Devetak examines the role of culture in an area which is intersected by state boundaries.

182　**New European countries and their minorities.**
　　C. D. Harris.　*Geographical Review*, vol. 83, no. 3 (1993), p. 301-20.
A brief outline of the position of ethnic minorities in Eastern Europe after the collapse of the Communist regimes, focusing on the successor states of Yugoslavia, Czechoslovakia and the USSR.

183　**Ethnic minorities in Slovenia.**
　　Edited by Boris Jesih, translated by Wayne Tuttle.　Ljubljana: Inštitut za narodnostna vprašanja, 1993. 58p.
Slovenia has official minorities of Italians in the coastal area and Hungarians in the east, as well as Yugoslavs and Gypsies. This book surveys the rights and position of the minorities in the light of the 1991 constitution.

184　**A joint Hungarian–Slovene research report concerning the situation of rural national minorities.**
　　R. Joo.　*Canadian Review of Studies in Nationalism*, vol. 13, no. 2 (1986), p. 9-14.
Joo examines the position of Hungarians within Slovenia, and the position of the Slovenes in four Hungarian villages.

185　**Kruh in politika.** (Bread and politics.)
　　Duša Krnel-Umek, Zmago Šmitek.　Ljubljana: Ethnic Group Studies, 1987. 780p.
Linguistically mixed communities were the norm before the First World War in some areas of the Alps. The authors present an ethnological survey of one of the few such surviving communities in Eastern Slovenia, the village of Vitanje from 1850 to 1940.

186　**Speaking Slovene – being Slovene – verbal codes and collective self images. Some correlations between Kanalska dolina and Žiljska dolina.**
　　Robert G. Minnich.　*Slovene Studies*, vol. 10, no. 2 (1988), p. 125-47.
Examines the relative role of language in the formation of collective self-understanding in villages at the intersection of the frontiers of Austria, Italy and Slovenia.

187　**Minorities in the Balkans.**
　　Hugh Poulton.　London: Minority Rights Group, 1991. 244p.
Important and meticulous study of the position of minorities in Southeastern Europe, including Slovenia.

188 **Slowenien und seine Gastarbeiter aus dem jugoslawischen Sueden.**
(Slovenia and its guest-workers from the south of Yugoslavia.)
B. Schmidt-Sakić. *Osteuropa*, vol. 40, no. 6 (1990), p. 367-76.

Slovenia had, and still has, a large number of citizens from the other Yugoslavian republics living and working in the republic, often doing the most menial and low-paid jobs. This article assesses the effect of these workers on Slovenian society and economy.

189 **According to the principle of reciprocity: the minorities in Yugoslav Austrian relations 1918-38.**
Arnold Suppan. In: *Ethnic groups in international relations.* Edited by Paul Smith, in collaboration with Kalliopi Koufa, Arnold Suppan. Dartmouth: New York University Press, European Science Foundation, 1991, p. 235-73.

This examination of the use of the 'Carinthian question' by Slovenian and German nationalists in the interwar years is written by a leading Austrian authority on Eastern European history.

190 **National linguistic minorities: bilingual basic education in Slovenia.**
Ela Ulrih-Atena. *Prospects*, vol. 6, no. 3 (1976), p. 430-8.

The author discusses the constitutional provision for ethnic Hungarians and Italians in Slovenia. The right to bilingual education was re-confirmed by the post-independence constitution of December 1991. See also Inka Štrukelj 'The dynamics of societal bilingualism: bilingual education in Slovenia', *Compare*, no. 1 (1978), p. 93-100.

191 **An ethnic mosaic – Austria before 1918.**
Sergij Vilfan. In: *Ethnic groups and language rights.* Edited by Sergij Vilfan, in collaboration with Gundmund Sandvik, Lode Wils. Dartmouth: New York University Press, European Science Foundation, 1993, p. 111-34.

Describes the transition of the Habsburg monarchy from a multi-ethnic empire to a collection of nations after 1918. Austria's rulers faced two main choices in governing these nations: assimilation by force or the 'protection of linguistic national diferences at all levels of public life'. The final century of the Habsburg monarchy is a history of this dilemma. Vilfan, a leading Slovenian scholar examines the government of the Austrian provinces during this time, with particular regard to the legal aspects of the problem.

Overseas Populations

Slovenes in the New World

192 **Slovene-Americans in Washington D.C.: a case of optional ethnicity.**
L. A. Bennett. *Slovene Studies*, vol. 8, no. 2 (1986), p. 21-30.
Discusses how Slovenes in the American capital opt either to be American or Slovene or a combination of these variables.

193 **Louis Adamič and the American dream.**
Henry A. Christian. *Journal of General Education*, vol. 27, no. 2 (Summer 1975), p. 113-23.
An interesting examination of the work of one of the most exciting writers of the twentieth century from the Slovene ethnic milieu. Oscar Handlin remarked that immigrants *are* American history. Therefore the life of Louis Adamič 'to a great degree is American history for his time' (p. 113).

194 **Perspectives on Slovene emigration to Argentina.**
Katica Čukjati. *Slovene Studies*, vol. 8, no. 2 (1986), p. 31-5.
More Slovenes emigrated to Argentina than to any other Latin American country. Here Čukjati assesses the Slovene cultural heritage in this setting, looking in particular at different generations and their attitudes.

195 **The Slovene-American press.**
J. D. Dwyer. In: *The ethnic press in the United States of America. A historical analysis and handbook.* Edited by S. M. Miller. New York: Greenwood Press, 1987, p. 369-78.
Dwyer looks at the role of newspapers such as *Ameriška Domovina* and *Edinost* for the Slovene community.

196 **The Slovene immigrant community in Argentina between the two world wars.**
R. Genorio. *Slovene Studies*, vol. 8, no. 2 (1986), p. 37-42.
Discusses the Slovene diaspora in Argentina and societies such as Ljudski oder (popular stage).

197 **Adjustment and assimilation of Slovenian refugees.**
Giles Edward Gobetz. New York: Arno Press, 1980. 203p.
(American Ethnic Groups Series: the European Heritage).
According to certain criteria, Slovenes would appear to be among the most assimilable groups in America. However, only 5.22 per cent of those questioned by Gobetz preferred to speak English over Slovene, although 94 per cent actually knew English. By culture, over half of respondents consider themselves to be Slovenians, less than 2 per cent entirely American, while the remainder saw themselves as mixed. Both Slovenia and America had a pull for those questioned, which suggests that they will remain as *Ameriški Slovenci* for some time to come. See also Gobetz's 'Slovenian ethnic studies', *Nationalities Papers*, vol. 2, no. 1 (1974), p. 19-26.

198 **Geographical distributions, age structure and comparative language maintenance of persons of Slovene language in the U.S.**
Toussaint Hočevar. New York: Society for Slovene Studies, 1978. 21p.
This comprehensive survey of Slovenes living in the United States was written by a prominent member of that community. Hočevar is also a distinguished economist.

199 **Sociolinguistic aspects of Slovene spoken in America.**
Joseph Paternost. *Slovene Studies*, vol. 1, no. 1 (1979), p. 14-24.
Discusses American Slovene as 'one of the many varieties of Slovene and as such has its own peculiarities in phonology and grammar, lexicon and semantic structure' (p. 15). For instance, when an American Slovene says *praktična katoličana*, meaning 'practising Catholics', a European Slovene would understand this as 'practical Catholics'. There are also many loanwords from English *kici* (kids) or *bil* (bill) and American Slovenes say *papir* instead of *časopis* for newspaper. In some industrial centres there is evidence of the development of Pan-Slavic *koine* (dialect), when Slovaks, Slovenes and Serbs get together. Nevertheless, Slovenes also assimilate by changing their names, so that *Erjavec* becomes Brown and *Zima* becomes Winters. See also Paternost's 'Slovenian language on Minnesota's iron range: some socio-linguistic aspects of language maintenance and language shift', *General Linguistics*, vol. 16, nos. 2-3 (1976), p. 95-150.

200 **Aspects of name changes among American Slovenes.**
Joseph Paternost. *Slovene Studies*, vol. 2, no. 2 (1980), p. 78-84.
Slovenes who came to America, particularly before the Second World War, were often pressurized or forced to change their names. Here, Joseph Paternost relates some of the curious tales as to how 'Znideršič' became 'Tagler', Omahen became 'O'Mahen' and 'Kraševec' became 'Wilson' (after the American President at that time).

201 **Problems in language contact and the social meaning of language among American Slovenes.**
Joseph Paternost. *Slovene Studies*, vol. 5, no. 2 (1983), p. 207-18.
Discusses the interference between American English and Slovene. For example, the Slovene verbs *znati, poznati* and *vedeti* can be translated by 'to know' in English and in this respect American Slovene 'suffers' through contact with the rather different linguistic concepts in English. The article includes an analysis of a dialogue.

202 **American ethonyms for Slovenians.**
David F. Stermole. *American Speech*, vol. 59, no. 3 (1984), p. 278-81.
Discusses American nicknames for Slovenes such as 'Greiner' and 'Windak', which were commonly adopted in a negative manner at the beginning of this century.

203 **Slovenians in Canada.**
Eleanot Tourtel, Peter Urbanc, design by Vinko Cekuta. Hamilton, Ontario: The Slovenian Heritage Festival Committee, 1984. 231p.
Designed to educate Canadian Slovenes in their 'own' culture, this book is packed with information both about the 'old country' and their immediate Canadian heritage. See also Rado Genorio, 'The post-war emigration of Slovenes to transatlantic countries: the Canadian case', *Florida University Slavic Papers*, vol. 5, no. 2 (1981), p. 106-18, and his more recent book, *Slovenci v Kanadi/Slovenes in Canada* (Ljubljana: Inštitut za geografijo Univerze Edvarda Kardelja, 1989. 184p.).

204 **The foundation of the Yugoslav Emergency Council in New York.**
Andrej Vovko. *Slovene Studies*, vol. 10, no. 2 (1988), p. 91-7.
Examines pro-Yugoslav activity in the United States during the Second World War. Of related interest is Bogdan Novak, 'Why Adamič shifted his support from Mihailović to Tito', *Slovene Studies*, vol. 11, nos. 1-2 (1989), p. 185-92.

205 **Metonymic metaphors and ethnicity: Slovenes in Cleveland.**
Irene P. Winner. *Slovene Studies*, vol. 9, nos. 1-2 (1987), p. 243-9.
Analyses the ethnographic position of Slovenes in the largest community in the USA from the perspective of the Peircean opposition of we:other. For the life history of a prominent Cleveland Slovene, see Ivan Molek, *Slovene immigrant history 1900-50, autobiographical sketches* (Dover, Delaware: Mary Molek Inc., 1979).

Slovenes in Austria and Italy

206 **The Jugoslavs of Italy.**
Fran Barbalić. *Slavonic and East European Review*, vol. 15, no. 43 (July 1936), p. 177-90.

Examines the position of the 650,000 ethnic Slovenes and Croats in the coastal areas that were incorporated into Italy after the First World War. In particular, he considers the fate of education and periodical publications under the Italians, as well as the fate of the religious. Barbalić quotes a few examples from a book published in Trieste in 1929 by Aldo Pizzagalli – *Per l'italianità dei cognomi* (How to Italianize surnames) – in which Čuk beomes Zucchi, Slavec changes to Salvi and Debeljak to Debelli. Barbalić concludes, 'by their annexation to Italy, the Jugoslav minority has lost its culture, its liberty, its daily bread and is in danger of losing the faith of its forefathers' (p. 188). See also *Racial minorities under Fascism in Italy* by Gaetano Salvamini (Chicago: [n.p.], 1934).

207 **The Slovene minority of Carinthia.**
Thomas M. Barker, with the collaboration of Andreas Moritsch.
Boulder, Colorado: East European Monographs; New York: Columbia University Press, 1984. 415p. maps. bibliog. (East European Monographs, no. 169).

The most comprehensive survey of the Slovene presence in Austrian Carinthia yet to be published in English. Although the book is rather brief about the medieval and early modern periods, it deals with the nineteenth and twentieth centuries in impressive detail, looking at the rise of German nationalism and the Slovene response.

208 **Social revolutionaries and secret agents: the Carinthian Slovene partisans and Britain's Special Operations Executive.**
Thomas M. Barker. Boulder, Colorado: East European Monographs; New York: Columbia University Press, 1990. xiii, 249p.

Looks at the resistance to Nazi rule which emerged in 1942 in the Slovene regions of the Third Reich and the involvement of British government agencies such as the Special Operations Executive (SOE) thereafter. See also Barker's 'The Ljubljana Gap strategy: alternative to Anvil/Dragoon or fantasy?', *Journal of Military History*, vol. 56 (Jan. 1992), p. 57-85; and 'Partisan warfare in the bilingual region of Carinthia', *Slovene Studies*, vol. 11, nos. 1-2 (1989), p. 193-210.

209 **The maintenance of bilingualism in Southern Austria.**
Lilyan A. Brudner. *Ethnology*, vol. 11, no. 1 (Jan. 1972), p. 39-54.

Charts the decline of 'Slavic' (i.e. Slovene) dialects in Carinthia since the Middle Ages, arguing that the decline of the *Gemeinde* (village council) after the mid-nineteenth century also increased the dominance of German. Brudner then continues by discussing the function of bilingualism in a socio-economic context.

210 **Successful negotiations: Trieste 1954: an appraisal by the five participants.**
Edited by John C. Campbell. Princeton, New Jersey: Princeton University Press, 1976. 181p. maps.

Interviews with five of the leading participants in the negotiations over Trieste after the Second World War, including Vladimir Velebit for Yugoslavia and Robert D. Murphy, who was American special envoy in Belgrade at the time. Other documents relating to the dispute over Trieste are also included. In 1975, the Treaty of Osimo finally settled the question of the border between Italy and Yugoslavia. This was published in English by Dopisna delavska univerza (Ljubljana, 1977. 93p.). Since independence, the Italian government has raised with with the Slovenian and Croatian authorities the question of the status of Istria and properties in Istria, which were deserted by the Italian *esuli* (exiles), but as yet no territorial changes or other concessions have been made.

211 **Life and death struggle of a national minority: the Jugoslavs in Italy.**
Lavo Čermelj, translated by Fanny S. Copeland. Ljubljana: Jugoslav Union of League of Nations Societies, 1936. 259p. (2nd ed., Ljubljana: Tiskarna ljudske pravice, 1945. 219p.).

Examines the plight of ethnic Slovenes and Croats in Italy during the interwar period, from a distinctly Yugoslavist cultural perspective.

212 **Venetian Slovenia.**
Lavo Čermelj. Belgrade: Yugoslav Institute for International Affairs, 1946. 22p. map.

Venetian Slovenia (Beneška Slovenija) is the term adopted to denote those parts of Italy, which were not part of the Habsburg monarchy where Slovenes lived. This short study, commissioned in the aftermath of the Second World War, looks at the ethnic character of this area.

213 **The race for Trieste.**
Geoffrey Cox. London: Kimber, 1977. 284p. maps.

In the spring of 1945, Geoffrey Cox was an intelligence officer serving with the New Zealand Division that advanced on Trieste to prevent a Communist takeover. Although Cox's work is generally antipathetic to the Yugoslavian cause, this is an important piece of scholarship from an eyewitness to the events. It is based on material available in the Public Record Office after the 25-year rule period elapsed.

214 **Symposium: the Slovenes of Northeastern Italy.**
James C. Davis, Jože Pirjevec, Aleš Lokar, Emidio Sussi.
Nationalities Papers, vol. 11, no. 2 (Fall 1983), p. 148-89.

Discusses the position of the Slovene minority in Italy, largely in Trieste and the villages of Eastern Friuli-Venezia-Giulia.

215 **The national development of the Carinthian Slovenes.**
Bogo Grafenauer. Ljubljana: Research Institute, Section for Frontier Questions, 1946. 91p.

A survey of the contraction of Slovene ethnic territory in the area that became the Austrian province of Carinthia after the First World War and the plebiscite of 1920.

216 **Ethnics in a borderland: an inquiry into the nature of ethnicity and reduction of ethnic tension in a one-time genocide area.**
Feliks Gross. Westport, Connecticut: Greenwood, 1978. 193p. map. bibliog.

Looks at the question of ethnic identity in the Julian region, which is divided between Italy and Slovenia and has ethnic groups speaking Friulian, Slovene, German and Italian. Some towns such as Tarvisio have no clear historical ethnic identity as they are essentially market-places with supra-national identity. As Gross remarks, this is an area of relative stability, although it was once characterized by extreme ethnic tension, especially in the first fifty years of this century.

217 **Chronological marriage patterns in Resia.**
Eric P. Hamp. *Slovene Studies*, vol. 10, no. 2 (1988), p. 201-2.

A lively summary and discussion of an article by Giovanni M. Rotta, 'La stagionalità dei matrimoni nella Valle di Resia (Udine) XVIII e XIX sec.', *Quaderni di Scienze Antropologiche*, no. 13 (1987), p. 110-45, which charts population decline in this fascinating 'Slovene' valley in Italy.

218 **The Slovenes of Italy and Austria.**
Janko Jeri. *Le Livre Slovène*, vol. 9, parts 3-4 (1973), p. 90-103.

A survey of the main historical events and the development of a national consciousness amongst the Slovene communities in Trieste and Carinthia.

219 **Harold Macmillan and the Cossacks: was there a Klagenfurt conspiracy?**
Robert Knight. *Intelligence and National Security*, 1 (1986), p. 234-54.

A polemic against Nikolai Tolstoy and his 'Klagenfurt conspiracy' thesis. For further criticism of Tolstoy's thesis see, Thomas M. Barker, 'A British variety of pseudo-history', in *Eisenhower and the German POWs*, edited by Stephen E. Ambrose and Guenther Bischof (Baton Rouge: Louisiana State University Press, 1992, p. 183-98).

220 **Robert Murphey's mission to Belgrade, September 1954 – the decisive step towards the final solution of the Trieste crisis: the evidence of the Foreign Ministry archives, Belgrade.**
Samo Kristen. *Slovene Studies*, vol. 12, no. 2 (1990), p. 157-68.

Looks at the diplomatic history of the final months of the 'Trieste Question'.

221 **Jan Badouin de Courtenay on the dialects spoken in Venetian Slovenia and Rezija.**
Rado L. Lenček. New York: Society for Slovene Studies, 1977. 43p.
A introduction to the work of the Polish linguist, who contributed a great deal to the study of Slavonic dialects through his fieldwork in the hills north of Udine in Italy.

222 **The Slovene minority in Italy from an economic perspective.**
Aleš Lokar, Marko Oblak. *Slovene Studies*, vol. 8, no. 1 (1986), p. 27-43.
Investigates the economic enterprises in which Slovenes in Italy are involved, and discusses the economic function of their bilingualism.

223 **Trieste and North Jugoslavia.**
Anton Melik. Ljubljana: Research Institute for Frontier Questions, 1946. 21p.
A polemical intervention into the Trieste Question from the Yugoslavian point of view. See also Melik's *Trieste and the littoral. A short geographical outline* (Ljubljana: Research Institute for Frontier Questions, 1946. 13p.).

224 **History teaching in Austria and Carinthia: a Slovene perspective.**
Andreas Moritsch. *Nationalities Papers*, vol. 7, no. 2 (1979), p. 147-53.
Discusses the way in which the history of ethnic Slovenes has been marginalized in the official history teaching in Austrian Carinthia. For an example of a Slovene history textbook designed for Carinthian school students, see Valentin Inžko, Z*godovina Slovencev: Od začetov do 1918* (A history of the Slovenes from the beginnings to 1908) (Celovec/Klagenfurt, Austria: Družba sv. Mohorja, 1978. 160p.).

225 **German nationalism and the Slovenes of Austria between the two world wars.**
Andreas Moritsch. *Slovene Studies*, vol. 8, no. 1 (1986), p. 15-20.
Discusses the role of extreme nationalist groups, such as the Kaerntner Heimatdienst and the Freiheitliche Partei and their links with contemporary extremism, particularly focused on Slovenes. This volume of *Slovene Studies* also contains a discussion by Peter Vodopivec: 'Commentary: the 1920 Carinthian plebiscite' (pages 21-5).

226 **Trieste, 1941-1954: the ethnic, political and ideological struggle.**
Bogdan C. Novak. Chicago: University of Chicago Press, 1970. 526p. maps. bibliog.
A grand survey of the Trieste Question during its most crucial phase by a widely repected American scholar of Slovene origin. For a more recent survey, see Osvaldo Croci, 'Search for parity: Italian and Yugoslav attitudes towards the question of Trieste', *Slovene Studies*, vol. 12, no. 2 (1991), p. 141-55.

227   **Variation on an alternation: the fate of the *kasna palatalizacija* in Šele Fara, Carinthia.**
Tom M. S. Priestly.   *Slovene Studies*, vol. 2 (1980), p. 63-77.

Šele Fara is a village with a population of approximately 830 inhabitants in Austrain Carinthia. All are fluent in German, and some in standard literary Slovene as well as their Slovene dialect. Based on the results of a field trip, Priestly makes the following observation: that one particular sound change is particularly important (i.e., the *kasna palatalizacija*) and he proceeds to study speech according to age, place of residence and gender.

228   **Cultural consciousness and political nationalism: language choice among Slovenes in Carinthia.**
Tom Priestly.   *Canadian Studies Review of Studies in Nationalism*, vol. 16 (1989), p. 78-97.

The Carinthian Slovenes are divided between feelings of ethnic loyalty to Slovenians and their economic roles and political citizenship within the Austrian Republic. Priestly discusses how choices are made about national self-consciousness.

229   **Between East and West: Trieste, the United States and the Cold War, 1941-1945.**
Roberto G. Rabel.   Durham, North Carolina; London: Duke University Press, 1988. 222p. maps.

Reviews the 'Trieste Question' from an international perspective.

230   **Trieste: ethnicity and the Cold War, 1945-54.**
Glenda Sluga.   *Journal of Contemporary History*, vol. 29, no. 2 (1994), p. 285-303.

Based on material from the Public Record Office in London and archives in Slovenia and Italy, this article reviews the Trieste Question from an ethnic perspective. Sluga argues that one of the effects of the Cold War was to equate 'Slavs' with Communism and to radicalize the Italian population of Trieste from the Slovenes and other South Slavs of the port and its hinterland. The 'discursive boundaries' between East and West still have repercussions in contemporary Triestine politics. For a more general discussion of the Trieste Question, see Charles Seton-Watson, 'Italy's Imperial hangover', *Journal of Contemporary History*, vol. 15 (1980), p. 169-79.

231   **No man's land: the gendered boundaries of post-war Trieste.**
Glenda Sluga.   *Gender and History*, vol. 6, no. 2 (Aug. 1994), p. 184-201.

Reviews the activities of women partisans and Communist supporters during the occupation period in Trieste. Sluga interviewed several elderly Slovene *drugarizzas* (women partisans) about their experience in Tito's Liberation Front. The ways in which contemporary observers, such as the New Zealander Geoffrey Cox, viewed the efforts of the Yugoslavs, particularly women, to rebuild the Adriatic port after the war are also discussed. Of related interest is Pavel Stranj, *The submerged community* (Trieste: Editoriale Stampa Triestina, 1992).

232 **The Slovene dialect of Resia San Georgio.**
Han Steenwijk. Atlanta, Georgia; Amsterdam: Rodopi Press, 1992.
352p. maps.

A detailed linguistic study of the Val Resia in northeastern Italy, where Slovene dialects have been preserved among the few thousand inhabitants. Much of the original fieldwork on the dialects of Resia was undertaken by the Polish scholar Jan Badouin de Courtenay in the nineteenth century and Steenwijk's study follows critically in his footsteps, testing many of the former's theories. This is one of the richest studies of the Slovene language in English and its clear, crisp style makes much of the content accessible, even for the non-specialist. The ethnographic content also makes the study relevant to students of peasant life. See also Steenwijk's 'The nominal declension of Friulian loans in the Slovene dialect of Val Resia', *Slovene Studies*, vol. 12, no. 1 (1990), p. 23-31.

233 **Resistance and the national question in the Venezia Giulia and Friuli.**
E. R. Terzuolo. In: *Nation and ideology. Essays in honor of Wayne C. Vucinich.* Edited by Ivo Banac, J. Ackermann, R. Szporluk.
Boulder, Colorado: Cornell University Press, 1981, p. 411-34.
(East European Monographs, no. 95).

Terzuolo looks from a political perspective at the struggle for the North East of Italy, an ethnically mixed area containing Italians, Slovenes and Croats.

234 **The maintenance of Slovenian in Carinthia: a Yugoslav–Austrian dispute.**
J. W. Tollefson. *Canadian Slavonic Papers*, vol. 23, no. 3 (1981), p. 302-14.

When Carinthians were consulted in October 1920 by the Interallied Plebiscite Commission, approximately 59 per cent chose the option of remaining under Austrian administration, while 41 per cent chose the Yugoslavian option. Since this time, the Slovene language has declined in Carinthia. The Austrian State Treaty of 1955 protects the rights of Slovene and Croat minorities, although as Tollefson points out, implementation of Article 7 (reproduced in the text) which 'involves the general call for bilingualism . . . has not been smooth' (p. 306). The various censuses conducted have also tended to split the community into 'Windisch' and 'Slovene'. Austria and its neighbour Yugoslavia had, according to Tollefson, 'differences in policy as well as fundamentally different interpretations of Carinthian history, the Austrian State Treaty, the role of censuses and the responsibility of the Austrian government for the minority population. The Austrian view is that historical factors and the terms of the State Treaty do not require any further support for Slovenians' (p. 313). See also Drago Drušković, *Carinthian Slovenes: some aspects of their situation* (Ljubljana: 1973).

235 **The Klagenfurt conspiracy: war crimes and diplomatic secrets.**
Nikolai Tolstoy. *Encounter*, vol. 60, no. 5 (May 1983), p. 24-37.

In an infamous article, Tolstoy discusses the fate of probably 10,000 Slovene Domobranci and other non-Communist Yugoslavs, who were murdered near Kočevje in the early summer of 1945 after they were transported over the Austrian border by the British authorities. Comparing the massacre to Katyn, Tolstoy assesses the culpability of General Charles Keightley, Toby Law (Lord Aldington) and Harold Macmillan, among others. This article also appeared in *South Slav Journal*, vol. 6, no. 1 (Spring 1983), p. 6-23, and was then presented as a full-length book, *The minister and the massacres* (London: Century Hutchinson, 1986. xxii, 442p.), which was subsequently withdrawn from libraries and bookshops after a protracted legal battle. A Croatian translation is still available.

236 **Drawing the line: Britain and the emergence of the Trieste Question, Jan 1941-May 1945.**
J. R. Whittam. *English Historical Review*, vol. 106, no. 2 (April 1991), p. 346-70.
Argues that the 'Trieste Question' did not appear suddenly in 1945, but that the Foreign Office had been concerned about the problems of this region for four years. Robin Laffan carried out a great deal of research at Balliol College, Oxford from 1941 onwards and there was a general agreement within the Foreign Office that the post-war frontier should be redrawn in favour of the Slovenes and Croats. During the next four years the situation was complicated by American and Soviet interventions. Roosevelt in particular wanted Trieste to be kept within Italy. Whittam considers the eventual resolution of the Trieste Question was 'perhaps the first significant success for the Western Allies in what was soon to be called the Cold War' (p. 370).

Languages and Dialects

General

237 **The formation of the Slovene literary language against the background of the Slavonic national revival.**
Robert Auty. *Slavonic and East European Review*, vol. 41, no. 2 (June 1963), p. 391-402.
Discusses the codification of standard Slovene in the nineteenth century from the perspective of Pan-Slavism and literary events in the wider Slavonic world.

238 **On the etymology of Beljak.**
Jakov Bačić. *Slovene Studies*, vol. 3, no. 1 (1981), p. 23-9.
The Carinthian town of Villach is known as Beljak in Slovene. Bačić argues that the *Urform* should be regarded as Belah and its meaning translated as either 'town on the white water' or 'the white town'. He goes on to argue that 'one of the oldest and commonest ways that the Indo-Europeans, and above all the Slavs, used to differentiate directionally opposed natural features and man-made features was to give those situated east of the observer and name-giver "red" or "black" and those west of him "white"' (p. 26).

239 **Towards an explanation of word order differences between Slovene and Serbo-Croat.**
David C. Bennett. *Slavonic and East European Review*, vol. 64, no. 1 (Jan. 1986), p. 1-24.
Word order varies greatly between the Slavonic languages, and its function has often been thought to be stylistic. By analysing the differences between a Slovene version of Ivan Cankar's *Bela križantema* (The white chrysanthemum), and a Serbo-Croat translation, Bennett makes some tentative observations on the differences in word order in the text. The novel is between 13,000 and 14,000 words long and word order differences are to be found in approximately 350 clauses. It is the clitics (unstressed

items) 'which are of particular interest to the word order of the two languages', although the author also discusses the position of verbs, adverbs and the position of the negative marker (*ne*) and the conditional marker (*bi*). When examining the behaviour of clitics in these two languages and their relationship to a common Slavonic 'it is useful to think in terms of the interaction of two kinds of constraints', the phonological and the semantic. In Slovene, unlike the common Slavonic, the semantic constraint is stronger than the phonological. Serbo-Croat may be progressing in the same direction as Slovene. Bennett also considers how the differences may have arisen. Slovene is more similar to the other languages in the Danube area, whereas Serbo-Croat is nearer to other Balkan languages, although this may be purely coincidental.

240 **Word order change in progress: the case of Slovene and Serbo-Croat and its relevance for Germanic.**
David C. Bennett. *Journal of Linguistics*, vol. 23, no. 2 (Sept. 1987), p. 269-87.
Bennett considers the influence of Germanic on Slovene and asks whether this can in part explain this language's differences from Serbo-Croat and how the data he gathered fits with established linguistic theory.

241 **Guide to the South Slavonic languages.**
Reginald G. A. de Bray. Columbus, Ohio: Slavica Publishers, 1980. 3rd ed. 399p. bibliog.
The 'standard reference work' (p. 7) for Slovene and the other South Slavonic languages, with grammatical and historical information. It is an invaluable work in a comparative context.

242 **Contemporary standard Slovene: a complex linguistic phenomenon.**
Daliber Brožović. *Slovene Studies*, vol. 10, no. 2 (1988), p. 175-90.
Contemporary standard Slovene can be characterized as having a large number of dialects in a small area and is in this respect perhaps the most extreme of the Slavonic languages. The article considers some of the different aspects of the standard language such as its dual (*dvojina*) and its Latin alphabet (*latinica*). Slovene has mixed Western and Southern Slavic characteristics, whereas Serbo-Croat has entirely Southern Slavonic characteristics. Brožović compares 59 words from Slovene with their equivalents in standard Slokavian Serbo-Croat. He then concludes that Slovene and Serbo-Croat, despite their differences, form one sub-group with the Southern Slavonic group.

243 **Aspects of adverbial placement in English and Slovene.**
Margaret G. Davis. Munich, Germany: Verlag Otto Sagner, 1989. 342p. (Series Slavistische Beitraege, Band 249).
A study of word order in linguistic theory, specifically comparing English and Slovene. English has a fairly fixed word order in so far as adverbs are concerned, whereas Slovene is far more fluid; the study proceeds to study the function of adverbial placement. A highly technical but accessible study, which is well written and nicely produced. Of related interest is Stefan Slak, 'Informational analysis of the

consonant–vowel sequence in Slovene', *Papers in Slovene Studies*, vol. 2 (1976), p. 165-78.

244 **Aspects of linguistic equality in Slovenia.**
Silvo Devetak. *Slovene Studies*, vol. 8, no. 2 (1986), p. 853-63.
A brief survey of the status of Slovene and minority languages in the Republic of Slovenia, based on data from the 1981 census. Devetak also includes the results of questionnaires about language use in shops, at work and at prayer.

245 **The relative chronology of the Slovene progressive stress shift.**
Ronald F. Feldstein. *Slovene Studies*, vol. 4, no. 2 (1982), p. 91-7.
Considers the theories of Ramovš, Jaksche and Stankiewicz on progressive stress shifts. 'The Slovene lengthening of non-rising vowels in newly closed syllables as well as the progressive shift of stress could be viewed as yet more evidence in favour of the existence of short-vowel pitch in early Slovene' (p. 95-6). See also Ruth A. Golush, 'The origin of vowel reduction in Slovene', *Papers in Slovene Studies*, vol. 2 (1976), p. 107-19.

246 **Some peculiarities of verbal aspect in Slovene.**
Herbert Galton. *Slovene Studies*, vol. 1, no. 2 (1979), p. 52-60.
A examination of word order in Slovene as compared to other Slavonic languages. See also Galton's 'The specific position of Slovene in the Slavic verbal aspect', *Slovene Studies*, vol. 3, no. 2 (1981), p. 49-58.

247 **Slovene and Serbo-Croatian place systems.**
Radmila Gorup. *Slovene Studies*, vol. 4, no. 1 (1982), p. 3-13.
A brief study which compares the distribution of cases and prepositions in Serbo-Croat and Slovene, with the aim of illustrating how these languages differ in what they say.

248 **On the dual inflections in Slovene.**
Eric Hamp. *Slavistična revija*, vol. 23, no. 1 (1975), p 67-70.
Discusses the use of the dual (*dvojina*) in Slovene, a subject which has attracted the interest of linguists looking at Slovene from a comparative Slavonic context.

249 **Solidarity, socialism and the Slovene second person singular.**
Zelimir B. Juričič, Joseph F. Kess. *Canadian Slavonic Papers*, vol. 20, no. 3 (Sept. 1978), p. 307-13.
Examines the occasions in which *ti* (you-familiar) and *vi* (you-formal and plural) are used in Slovenia and Croatia, comparing this with Russian and French usage. Also notes that terms like *kolegica* (female colleague) are used as an intermediary form of address. See also – by the same authors – 'Slovene pronominal address forms: rural vs. urbal sociolinguistic strategies', *Anthropological Linguistics*, vol. 20, no. 7 (1978), p. 297-311.

250 **Slovene neo-circumflex.**
Frederik H. H. Kortlandt. *Slavonic and East European Review*, vol. 54, no. 1 (1976), p. 1-10.
Kortlandt argues that the rise of the neo-circumflex came after the dissolution of Slavonic linguistic unity (p. 1). He then applies this observation to the study of Slovene.

251 **On dilemmas and compromises in the evolution of modern Slovene.**
Rado L. Lenček. In: *Slavic linguistics and language teaching.* Edited by Thomas F. Magner. Cambridge, Massachusetts: [n.p.], 1976, p. 112-52.
Discusses the history of the Slovene language from the point of view of a language teacher and scholar.

252 **The structure and history of the Slovene language.**
Rado L. Lenček. Columbus, Ohio: Slavica Publishers, 1982. 365p. maps. bibliog.
Lenček, a leading American Slovene, gives a historical background to the formation of Slovene as a distinctive Slavonic language, then proceeds to discuss dialectical variations and contemporary standard Slovene. An indispensable guide for anyone attempting to learn the language, or indeed to understand the evolution of Slovene national culture. The book also contains a bibliography of extant Slovene texts before the rise of mass publishing in the late eighteenth century.

253 **To honor Jernej Kopitar 1780-1980.**
Edited by Rado L. Lenček, Henry R. Cooper, Jr. Ann Arbor: Michigan Slavic Publication, 1982. 256p. (Papers in Slavic Philology, no. 2).
A collection of scholarly articles, which consider the impact of the work of the librarian and scholar Jernej Kopitar, whose influence on the formation of Slovenian national consciousness was crucial, particularly as Kopitar distinguished between the Slovene and Serb speech areas, but had very little regard for the separate existence of a Croat language. Of related interest is Sergio Bonazza, 'Jernej Kopitar: his place in Slovene cultural history', in: *Juraj Križanić (1618-83) Russophile and ecumenic visionary.* Edited by Thomas Eekman and Ante Kadić (The Hague: Mouton, 1976, p. 179-83).

254 **Analogy in the accentological history of conservative Slovene.**
Lew R. Micklesen. *Slovene Studies*, vol. 2, no. 1 (1980), p. 3-14.
Dealing with the salient developments of conservative Slovene (based on the dialects of central Lower Carniola and southern Upper Carniola, including Ljubljana), Micklesen argues that it is necessary to go back to the 'pre-history of Slavic' (p. 30) to investigate the opposition between rising and falling pitch on long initial syllables. Although the intonational history of conservative standard Slovene is still not entirely clear, 'it can be argued quite effectively that all the changes touched upon are analogical responses to just three phonological moments in the history of the language: the reduction of stress to a laryngealised or long syllable, the retraction of

stress to the initial mora of the word, and the retraction of stress occasioned by the loss of weak jers, aided and abetted, of course, by the preservation of length only in immediately pretonic syllables' (p. 13-14).

255 Form and function in the peripheral cases in Slovene dialects: some preliminary observations.
Raymond Miller. *Slovene Studies*, vol. 12, no. 1 (1990), p. 5-22.

Discusses the morphlogy of three peripheral cases – dative, locative and instrumental – in selected Slovene dialects, using models developed by the linguist Roman Jakobson in the 1950s. See also Vladimir Rehak, 'Classes of morphological change in Slovenian', *Slavic and East European Journal*, vol. 11, no. 2 (1967), p. 191-5.

256 Problems in the creation of an orthography: functional load, interference and political preferences.
T. M. S. Priestly. *Slavic and East European Journal*, vol. 36, no. 3 (Fall 1992), p. 302-16.

Looks at the phonology of Selsq, the dialect of Šele in Austrian Carinthia.

257 The maintenance of national languages in a socialist setting: Slovene in Yugoslavia.
Dimitrij Rupel. *Slovene Studies*, vol. 8, no. 2 (1986), p. 43-52.

'To put it bluntly, in Yugoslavia, Slovene is a second class language' (p. 47). Rupel outlines how Slovenes had to learn Serbo-Croat to have a citizen's relation with the state, and how the heterogeneous nature of the Republic was threatened by increasing use of Serbo-Croat. An interesting piece of 'history', which can now be read in a different context.

258 The Slavic literary languages: formation and development.
Edited by Alexander M. Schenker, Edward Stankiewicz. Columbus, Ohio: Slavica Publishers, 1980. 287p. (Yale Russian and East European Publications, no. 1).

The chapter 'Slovenian' (p. 85-102) by Edward Stankiewicz, provides a basic historical outline on the development of Slovene as a literary language, which includes summaries of the views of early writers on the role of their language. The Protestant reformer Primož Trubar refused to remove Germanisms from his Slovene on the grounds that his writings were only for the Slovenes and 'not for Croats, Bezjaks, Bohemians or Poles' (p. 89). Stankiewicz indicates that the development of a literary language, far from being an organic process was influenced by the preconceptions of linguists such as Jernej Kopitar who believed that the Slavonic languages were dialects like the Greek *koine* and would one day be merged into a single tongue. Others, such as Stanko Vraz saw the Slovene language as being part of an Illyrian family which influenced in turn their political orientation. After the Serb-Croat literary agreement in 1850, 'the enrichment of the literary language was no longer conceived in terms of the creation of a mixed Slavic language, but rather as the harmonious adaptation of foreign Slavic words to Slovenian' (p. 100). For more specialist studies by Edward Stankiewicz, see: 'The prosodic system of the Slovenian declension', *Zbornik za filologiju i lingvistiku*, vol. 11 (1968), p. 257-66; 'The vocalic systems of modern standard Slovenian', *International Journal of Slavic Linguistics and Poetics*, vol. 1-2 (1959), p. 70-6; and 'Accent and vowel alternations in the substantive declension of modern standard Slovenian', *Slavic and East European Journal*, vol. 3, no. 2 (1959), p. 144-59.

259 **Morpho-syntatic expansions in translation from English into Slovenian as a prototypical response to the complexity of the original.**
Milena Milojević Sheppard. Munich: Verlag Otto Sagner, 1993. 254p. (Series Slavistische Beitraege, no. 306).

A very technical piece of translation theory, which concentrates on the English text of Agatha Christie's *Cat among the pigeons* and its Slovene translation by Zoja Skušek Močnik, *Mačka med golobičkami*. The author considers various types of 'complexity' for translation such as the formal and semantic, as well as the 'complexity' of the original. For further reading, see also Nada Sabec, 'Functional and structural constraints on Slovene–English code-switching', *Slovene Studies*, vol. 10, no. 1 (1988), p. 71-80.

260 **Word accent and vowel duration in standard Slovene: an acoustic and linguistic investigation.**
Tatjana Srebot-Rejec. Munich: Verlag Otto Sagner, 1988. 286p. (Series Slavistische Beitraege, no. 226).

The aim of this detailed empirical study was to examine the basic aspects of vowel duration in Slovene. The study begins with a survey of previous work on Slovene tonematics. Srebot-Rejec's investigation involves looking at the speech patterns of several standard Slovene speakers, who were chosen completely at random in 1981 ands 1982. The well-known linguists Tine Logar and Urska Snedič were then asked to interpret the data. This is a specialized, but also highly scholarly piece of work, which should be of methodological significance to readers beyond the field of tonematics. See also Ilse Lehiste, 'The phonemes of Slovene', *International Journal of Slavic Linguistics and Poetics*, vol. 4 (1961), p. 48-66.

261 **J. W. Valvasor's *Ehre des Herzogthums Krain* (1689): a source for the history of the Slovene language.**
Gerald Stone. *Slovene Studies*, vol. 12, no. 1 (1990), p. 43-54.

Stone argues that the work of J. W. Valvasor is a neglected source for the study of the Slovene language during a period where relatively few sources for language exist. Although the Carniolan Baron wrote in German, there are copious Slovene words in the text of *Die Ehre des Herzogthums Krain* (The honour of the Duchy of Carniola), including fifty different names for birds. Valvasor even wrote complete sentences in Slovene, indicating that for him the Slovene language fulfilled an intellectual function rather than being solely a language of translation, and perhaps that he sometimes spoke to himself in the language.

262 **Jan Kollar's thesis of Slavic reciprocity and the convergence of the intellectual vocabularies of the Czech, Slovak, Slovene, Croatian and Serbian standard languages.**
George Thomas. *Canadian Slavonic Papers*, vol. 34, no. 3 (1992), p. 279-99.

Looks at the influence of the Slovak poet and Pan-Slavist Jan Kollar (1793-1852) on the nineteenth-century linguistic exchanges between the Slavonic languages. See also his 'The Slavisation of the Slovene and Croatian lexicons. Problems in their inter-relationships', *Slovene Studies*, vol. 9 (1987), p. 217-25, and Karol Gadanyi, 'From the history of Slovene 19th century lexicography', *Slovene Studies*, vol. 14, no. 1 (1992), p. 3-8.

263 **The language situation and language policy in Slovenia.**
James W. Tollefson. Washington, DC: University Press of America, 1981. 285p. bibliog.

Examines language policy in Slovenia from the perspective of the Yugoslavian conception of nationality and language. Not only does Tollefson provide a useful historical introduction to the Slovene language but he also looks at some socio-economic aspects of Slovene. He concluded that the maintenance of Slovene was vital to the continuation of the Yugoslavian Federation. This book is a revised version of Tollefson's PhD dissertation, 'Diglossia and language policy, with special reference to Slovenia' (Stanford University, 1978. 346p.).

264 **A language of a small nationality (Slovene) in a multilingual state.**
Jože Toporišič. In: *Sociolinguistic problems in Czechoslovakia, Hungary, Romania and Yugoslavia.* Edited by William R. Schmalstieg, Thomas F. Magner. *Folia Slavica*, vol. 1, no. 3 (1978), p. 480-6.

Reflects the concern about the status of Slovene from one of the country's leading linguists. What, asked Toporišič, are the long-term consequences of Slovene/Serbo-Croat bilingualism were the latter to become a lingua communis? How would the influx of Serbo-Croat speakers into the tiny republic influence Slovene? With great prescience, Toporišič claimed that the Slovenes would either continue to assimilate linguistically, become a minority within Slovenia or change the nature of their relationship with their southern neighbours.

Dictionaries

265 **Angleško–Slovenski slikovni slovar.** (English–Slovene picture dictionary.)
Sonja Berce, Milena Hajnšek-Holz, Borislava Kosmrlj-Levačič, Andrej Novak. Oxford: Clarendon Press; Ljubljana: Cankarjeva založba, 1989. 862p.

This picture dictionary, containing 28,000 subject entries, enables the English- or Slovene-speaking reader to identify precisely the desired word.

266 **Etimološki slovar slovenskega jezika, I.** (Etymological dictionary of the Slovene language, Vol. I.)
France Bezlaj. Ljubljana: Mladinska knjiga/Slovenska akademija znanosti in umetnosti, 1976. 235p.

The leading source for Slovene etymology. The first volume of this dictionary covers the letters A-J. Volume II, covering K-O, appeared from the same publishers in 1982 (265p.) but Bezlaj died before he could complete his *magnum opus*.

267 **Slovensko–Angleški slovar.** (Slovene–English dictionary.)
Anton Grad, Henry Leeming. Ljubljana: Državna založba Slovenije, 1993. 827p.

The standard Slovene–English dictionary, revised and improved by the leading scholar Harry Leeming.

268 **Veliki Angleško–Slovenski slovar.** (Large English–Slovene dictionary.)
Anton Grad, Ruzena Skerlj, Nada Vitorović. Ljubljana: Državna založba Slovenije, 1992. 1377p.

The standard English–Slovene dictionary.

269 **English Slovene and Slovene English dictionary.**
Daša Komač, Ružena Skerlj. Ljubljana: Cankarjeva založba, 1985. 7th ed. 787p.

A compact but substantial dictionary, containing around 100,000 words in each language. Ideal for either the student or the traveller.

270 **Woerterbuch des deutschen Sprachinselmundart von Zarz/Sorica und Deutschrut/Rut in Jugoslawien.** (Dictionary of the German dialects in the linguistic islands of Sorica and Rut in Yugoslavia.)
Eberhard Kranzmejer, Primus Lessiak, edited by Maria Hornung, Alfred Ogris. Klagenfurt, Austria: Verlag des Geschichtsvereins fuer Kaernten, 1983. xvi, 193p.

The Slovene lands contained many German linguistic islands, where the people spoke dialects which were often archaic and only dimly comprehensible to speakers of standard German. The biggest such population was in Kočevje in southern Slovenia. This dictionary records the dialects of Sorica and of Rut near Tolmin as they were spoken in the interwar period.

271 **Slowenisch–Deutsch–Lateinisches Woerterbuch.** (Slovene–German–Latin dictionary.)
Hieronym Megister, edited by Annelies Laegreid. Wiesbaden, Germany: Otto Harrassowitz, 1967. 385p.

A facsimile of a trilingual dictionary that first appeared in 1592, with a modern translation. For Italian speakers a similar dictionary was produced by Gregorio Alasia da Sommaripa, *Vocabolario italiano–sloveno, altri testi italiano–sloveni e testi sloveni, Udine 1607.* Introduced by Lino Legiša (Ljubljana [Duino/Auresina/Trieste]: Mladinska knjiga, 1979. 311p.).

272 **Slovenian–English glossary of linguistic terms.**
Joseph Paternost. [n.p.]: Pennsylvania State University Publications, 1966. 339p.

For those who have failed to find a term in a standard dictionary, this book arranged thematically rather than alphabetically provides useful specialist vocabulary, which would be of particular help to those attempting to translate Slovene texts.

Grammars

273 **A concise grammar of Slovene.**
George Carcas. Pontypridd, Wales: Languages Information Centre, 1994. 36p.

A brief and jocular introduction to the basics of Slovene grammar, which the author hopes will encourage the reader to 'seek a deeper knowledge of one of the earliest recorded Slavonic languages' (p. 1).

274 **A basic reference grammar of Slovene.**
William W. Derbyshire. Columbus, Ohio: Slavica Publishers, 1993. 154p.

Designed for English-language native speakers who are at either an elementary or intermediate level of language acquisition, the book covers all the main points of Slovene grammer, with an English translation and explanatory text throughout. One of the best introductions to Slovene grammar, it covers the aspects that English native speakers find particularly difficult, such as word accent.

275 **Slovene for travellers.**
Miran Hladnik, Toussaint Hočevar. Ljubljana: Feniks, 1988. 120p.

A phrase-book with essential tips for travellers in Slovenia, accompanied by two audio-cassettes.

276   **Slovenscina za tujce.** (Slovene for foreigners.)
      Hermina Jug-Krajec.   Ljubljana: Pleško, 1989. 326p. 2 cassettes. map.
This is both an accessible and a scholarly language course. All vocabulary can be
found in an English-language glossary at the end of the book, but the text is entirely in
Slovene. The book is accompanied by two lively cassettes of the individual lessons.

277   **Slovenščina/ Slovene: a self-study course.**
      Programmed and designed by Manja Skrubej.   Ljubljana: RTV
      Ljubljana, 1983. 3 vols.
This Slovene audio language course in twenty lessons consists of: two books of texts
and translations with exercise models; a third booklet containing vocabulary and
exercises relating to the twelve tapes which form the basis of the course. The
emphasis is on conversation rather than grammar, which makes this an ideal course
for the non-specialist.

278   **Zakaj ne po slovensko?** (Why not [speak] in Slovene?)
      Jože Toporišič.   Ljubljana: Slovenska izseljenska matica, 1970.
      272p. 6 records.
A course to please grammatical and linguistic purists. Joze Toporišič's pedagogic
approach can be recommended to those who have studied languages in some depth
before, but it is less accessible for the complete beginner.

Religion

279 Religious art in Slovenia.
Jože Anderlič, Marjan Zadnikar, translated by Danica Dolenc, edited
by Marija Briški. Koper, Slovenia: Ognjišče, 1986. 272p.

Consisting mainly of coloured illustrations, this is a guide to some of the highlights of
art in churches and galleries in Slovenia, including the marvellous fifteenth-century
frescos at Hrastovlje, which depict amongst other things the 'dance of death'. See also
Marjan Zadnikar, *Hrastovlje: Romanska arhitektura in gotske freske* (Hrastovlje:
Romanesque architecture and Gothic frescos) (Ljubljana: Družina, 1988. 199p.). The
latter has a summary in English (p. 175-85).

280 The religious life of the Slovene in Australia.
Breda Čebulj-Sajko. *Slovene Studies*, vol. 14, no. 2 (1992),
p. 185-203.

Although the Catholic Church in Australia was established primarily to look after the
needs of Irish emigrants, a 1981 census indicated that only 7 per cent of Australian
Catholics are of Anglo-Celtic origins. Australia now has three main Slovene religious
centres: Kew, Melbourne; Marylands, Sydney; and Adelaide; and has its own
organization Planica. Breda Čebulj-Sajko traces the emigration of Slovenes to
Australia since the nineteenth century. In 1953 two priests established the journal
Misli, which in 1991 had a print run of 2,000. The work of the Franciscan order is
seen as being particularly important.

281 The priestly leaders of the Slovenes.
Elizabeth Christitch. *Ecclesiastical Review* (Philadelphia), vol. 50
(1919), p. 363-71.

An examination of the religious state of the Slovenes, and in particular the role of the
Bishop of Ljubljana after the First World War.

282 **Gutenberg, humanism, the Reformation and the emergence of the Slovene literary language, 1550-1584.**
Martin Dimnik. *Canadian Slavonic Papers*, vol. 26, nos. 2-3 (June-Sept. 1984), p. 141-59.

Discusses the relationship between humanism, printing and the production of Slovene-language texts in the mid-sixteenth century. Dimnik feels that the figure of the Triestine Bishop Peter Bonomo was particularly important as a bridge between humanist literary culture and the spread of Protestant ideas, in that he was the mentor of Primož Trubar, the most important figure in the Slovene Reformation. Trubar and his later followers, including Jurij Dalmatin, then went on to produce a Slovene-language catechism (1550) and a Bible (1584) which were published in Germany. The first Slovene printer Janez Mandelc printed a vernacular version of the first five books of the Old Testament in 1578, but was later expelled on religious grounds from Ljubljana by the Habsburg emperor.

283 **Primož Trubar and the mission to the South Slavs.**
Martin Dimnik. *Slavonic and East European Review*, vol. 66, no. 3 (July 1988), p. 380-99.

Looks at the life of the most important Slovene Protestant reformer, Primož Trubar. While living as a preacher in Bavaria, Trubar encouraged the production of several religious texts in Slovene. He also oversaw the largely unsuccessful attempts to produce religious material for *glagolaši* (those South Slavs who used the Glagolitic alphabet). Dimnik argues that Trubar is significant not only because he influenced the formation of the Slovene literary language, but also in the early discussions concerning the creation of a unified South Slav idiom based on the Bosnian dialect known as *ikavska štokavština*.

284 **The attitude of the Slovene Catholic Church to emigration to the United States of America before 1914.**
Marjan Drnovšek. *Slovene Studies*, vol. 14, no. 2 (1992), p. 169-84.

According to demographers and historians some 250,000-300,000 people emigrated from the Slovene lands before 1914, mostly to North and South America. Drnovšek assesses the attitude of the Catholic Church to the emigration of its flock, including a discussion of the Slovene Catholic Congresses in 1892, 1900 and 1906 and the Slovene-Croat Congress of 1913. Darko Friš also gives 'A brief survey of the activities of the Catholic Church among Slovene immigrants in the U.S.A. (1871-1941)' in *Slovene Studies*, vol. 14, no. 2 (1992), p. 205-16.

285 **Friderik Baraga: a portrait of the first bishop of Marquette based on the archives of the Congregatio de Propaganda Fide.**
Maksimilijan Jezernik. New York, Washington: Studia Slovenica, 1968. 155p.

Friderik Irenej Baraga was born in Mala vas (Dobrnic) in the Slovene lands in 1797 and trained in theology in Ljubljana and in law in Vienna. He went to the United States to undertake missionary work in 1830 after serving as a priest in Ljubljana and he worked for 37 years covering an immense stretch of territory around Lake Superior in Ottawa, amongst the native Americans. In 1855, he became Bishop of Toronto, with responsibility for all native peoples. He published many books about native

American languages and a history of the North American Indians, *Abrégé de l'histoire des Indiens de l'Amérique septentrionale* (Paris: E. J. Bailly, 1837. 296p.). Jezernik's clearly written protrait of this saintly man should be of interest to ethnologists, as well as to linguists and theologians.

286   **The official journal of the missionary expedition in 1849-50.**
Ignacij Knoblehar.   In: *The opening of the Nile Basin.*   Edited by
Elias Toniolo.   New York: Barnes and Noble, 1975, p. 47-54.

The journal of a Slovene missionary in Africa, who journeyed up the Nile in 1850. On the ethnographic importance of Knoblehar, see Zmago Šmitek, *Klic dalnjih svetov. Slovenci in neevropske kulture* (The call of distant worlds. The Slovenes and non-European cultures) (Ljubljana: Založba Borec, 1986. 359p.). It has an English summary on pages 325-48.

287   **Franc Pirc as peacemaker during the Sioux uprising of 1862.**
E. A. Kovačič.   *Slovene Studies*, vol. 8, no. 2 (1986), p. 15-19.

Born in Ljubljana in 1785, Pirc made his way to the Michigan area in 1835 where he remained as a missionary until 1873, before returning to his native town, where he died in 1880. Kovačič argues that his empathy with native American culture (which was partly inspired by Bishop Baraga) made him a crucial intermediary in 1862. See also A. K. Donchenko, 'Slovene missionaries in the Upper Midwest', in *The Other Catholics*. Edited by K. P. Dyrud (New York: Arno, 1978, p. 1-22).

288   **Christian Democracy in Yugoslavia: Slovenia.**
Miha Krek.   In: *Christian Democracy in Central Europe.*   New
York: Christian Democratic Union of Central Europe, 1952, p. 65-76.

A brief survey of the state of Christian Democracy during the early years of the Communist regime.

289   **Primus Trubar and the Slovene Protestant reformation.**
Branka Lapajne.   PhD dissertation, Institute of Historical Research,
University of London, 1980. 325p.

A comprehensive biography of the leading Slovene Protestant reformer and his work. Excellently presented and containing much original research, this thesis is also a good introduction to the early modern history of this region.

290   **The two divergent ideological concepts underlying the language concepts of Croatian and Slovene Protestant writers.**
Olga Nedeljković.   *Slovene Studies*, vol. 8, no. 1 (1986), p. 57-72.

Nedeljković argues that whereas the Slovenes forged a new language to 'create God's word', the Croats adopted their existing language for theological purposes. See also, by the same author, 'Illyrian humanist ideals in the work of South Slavic publishers in Urach', *Slovene Studies*, vol. 6, nos. 1-2 (1984), p. 127-42.

291 **Evangelini: the Protestant intermezzo in Žužemberk.**
Irma M. Ožbalt. *Slovene Studies*, vol. 6, nos. 1-2 (1984), p. 191-201.

Drawing on the unpublished manuscript, *Zgodbe župnije Žužemberk* (History of the parish of Žužemberk), written by the priest Alojž Županc in 1958, Ožbalt recreates some of the flavour of the religious and cultural flux in Dolenjska at the end of the sixteenth century. Protestantism was brought to the town by the Count Auersberg Herbart and his son Andrej. After a Lutheran predicant Kristof Slivec was installed in 1580, the town became religiously divided, the Church of St James remaining Catholic, while the Church of St Nicolas was run by the 'evangelini'. Although the Counter-reformation and the visitation of the Inquisition eventually drove the Protestants out, or to take measures of passive resistance, a few remnants of this period remain in the local memory up to the twentieth century, including references to the 'Protestant church' and the house name 'Evangelin'.

292 **Protestantism and the emergence of Slovene literature.**
Boris Paternu. *Slovene Studies*, vol. 6, nos. 1-2 (1984), p. 73-91.

The Slovene language was first codified by Protestant writers in the sixteenth century. They endeavoured to translate religious literature into the vernacular. Paternu, a leading literary scholar from Ljubljana, discusses the subsequent effect of this efflorescence of Slovene printing on the work of littérateurs in the nineteenth century, such as Jernej Kopitar and France Prešeren.

293 **Pisma Primoža Trubarja.** (The letters of Primus (Primož) Trubar.)
Edited by Jože Rajhman. Ljubljana: Slovenska akademija znanosti in umetnosti, 1986. 375p.

A complete edition of Primož Trubar's letters concerning religious reform in the sixteenth century. The letters appear in their original German form with Slovene translations. See also Rajhman's 'Jurij Dalmatin and his Bible in the light of literary history and theology', *Slovene Studies*, vol. 6, nos. 1-2 (1984), p. 113-25.

294 **A Marxist looks at the 16th century: Edvard Kardelj's view of the Slovene Reformation.**
Carole Rogel. *Slovene Studies*, vol. 6, no. 1-2 (1984), p. 49-54.

Rogel considers the role of Marxist theory in Kardelj's evaluation of the national significance of the first use of the Slovene language by Protestant reformers and the peasant uprisings in the sixteenth century when the peasants demanded *Stara prava!* (ancient rights!)

295 **The Protestant movement of Slovenes in Pannonia.**
Franc Sebjanić, translated by Susanne Kiraly-Moss. Murska sobota, Slovenia: Pomurska založba, 1978. 59p.

Protestantism remained in the far eastern corner of the Slovene lands after the Counter-reformation in the early seventeenth century all but wiped it out elsewhere. Here, Sebjanić tells the story of this tiny community that survived because of relative tolerance on the part of the Hungarians.

Social Conditions

Social strata and social problems

296 Redomestication of Slovene women.
Majca Jogan. *Women's Studies International Forum*, vol. 17, no. 2/3
(March-June 1994), p. 307-10.

Examines the impact of the political changes since 1991 on women's lives, including
the 'rechristanisation' of Slovenian public life and the social mores of the Christian
Democrats.

**297 Alcohol consumption among junior high school students in the
community of Litija.**
M. Kolšek. *Journal of Studies on Alcohol*, vol. 55, no. 1 (1994),
p. 55-60.

Kolšek looks at the phenomenon of teenage drinking in a small community in rural
Slovenia. It is seen to be high compared with their urban counterparts.

**298 Refugee perception of their situation the case of Croatian refugees
in Slovenia.**
M. Polič, A. Bauman, Z. Bukinac, V. Rajh, B. Ušeničnik.
International Journal of Psychology, vol. 27, nos. 3-4 (1992),
p. 314-15.

Abstract of a paper delivered at the 25th International Congress of Psychology in
Brussels, 19-24 July 1992.

299 Yugoslavia in turmoil: after self-management.
Edited by James Simmie, Jože Dekleva. London: Pinter, 1991. 167p.

An important collection of essays that consider the social problems of Yugoslavia in
transition, including 'From the new social movements to political parties' (p. 45-64)
by the well-known Slovenian writer Tomaž Mastnak.

300 **Social policy in Slovenia – between tradition and innovation.**
Edited by Ivan Svetlik. Aldershot, England: Avebury, 1992. 138p.
maps. (Studies in the Social Policy of Eastern Europe and the Soviet
Union Series).

An extremely comprehensive and well set-out introduction to social policy issues in
Slovenia, which should currently be regarded at the major text in the field. Katja Boh
(p. 84-93) discusses reform issues of the healthcare system, while Nevenka Černigoj-
Sadar and Maja Vojnović consider childcare policy (p. 94-107). The volume is edited
by the Head of the Centre of Welfare Studies in Ljubljana, whose main preoccupation
has been with researching into the quality of life. There is also an excellent historical
introduction by the editor (p. 1-14) and a theoretical discussion of the problems of
transition to a post-socialist society by Zinka Kolavić (p. 15-32).

301 **Reform of social policy in Slovenia – a soft approach.**
Ivan Svetlik. *Journal of European Social Policy*, vol. 3, no. 3 (1993),
p. 195-208.

Reviews the nature of the changes to social policy in Slovenia since 1990.

Social and cultural theory

302 **Democracy between tyranny and liberty: women in post-'socialist'
Slovenia.**
Milica G. Antić. *Feminist Review*, no. 39 (1991), p. 149-54.

Special issue entitled 'Shifting territories: feminism and Europe'. Although there was
an identifiable women's movement in Yugoslavia after the 1970s, because of widely
disparate development between the regions, women faced different problems. Antić
criticizes the 'big subject' in contemporary politics, namely nationalism and reminds
the reader that after the first democratic and free elections in April 1990 the
percentage of women in parliament declined from 25 per cent to 10 per cent. She
discusses the arrangements for women in the new constitution and the backlash of the
Christian Democrats, who wanted to end abortion rights.

303 **The sublime theorist of Slovenia (an interview with Slavoj Žižek).**
Peter Canning. *Artforum*, vol. 31, no. 7 (1993), p. 84-9.

Žižek, one of the most widely read Slovenian authors in the West and author of *The
sublime object of ideology* (London: Verso, 1989. xvi, 240p.), is interviewed here in a
stylish large-format art magazine.

304 **Lacan in Slovenia – an interview with Slavoj Žižek and Renata Salecl.**
Peter Dews, Peter Osborne. *Radical Philosophy*, vol. 19, no. 2 (Summer 1991), p. 25-31.
Renata Salecl and Slavoj Žižek, two of the leading intellectuals of the younger generation in Slovenia are interviewed here about their views on Lacanian psychoanalysis and the political situation in the former Yugoslavia. An interesting discussion of theory and praxis.

305 **The spoils of freedom: psychoanalysis and feminism after the fall of socialism.**
Renata Salecl. London: Routledge, 1994. vii, 167p.
This account of the situation for women after the end of the Communist regimes is written by one of Slovenia's leading cultural critics.

Social Services, Health and Welfare

306 **Antihormones in health and disease.**
Edited by M. K. Agarwal.   Basel: Karger, 1991. 200p.
Proceedings of a satellite symposium of the 2nd European Congress of Endocrinology in Ljubljana in 1990.

307 **Long term IUD use in Ljubljana, Yugoslavia.**
Lidija Andolšek.   Durham, North Carolina: Family Health
International, 1988. xiii, 81p.
An illustrated survey of contraceptive use in Ljubljana, assessing the success and social acceptability of intrauterine devices. See also B. Pinter, 'Continuation of contraceptive use in Slovenia. Life table analysis', *European Journal of Obstetrics Gynecology and Reproductive Biology*, vol. 55, no. 1 (1994), p. 54. Lidija Andolšek is also the author of *The Ljubljana Abortion Study 1971-73* (Bethesda: National Institute of Health, Center for Population Research, 1974. 57p.).

308 **The other side of employed parents' life in Slovenia.**
Nevenka Černigoj-Sadar.   *Marriage and the Family Review*, vol. 14, nos. 1-2 (1989), p. 69-80.
Although the provision of nursery education in Slovenia is excellent and many working parents can rely on an extended family for help, many families still experience stress when coping with the joint demands of career and family life, as well as deepening economic problems in the Slovenian case. These general problems are discussed here with the added note that Slovenes placed a very high value on the quality of family life.

309 **Health care planning in Slovenia.**
Robert G. Dyck.   *Papers in Slovene Studies*, vol. 3 (1977), p. 105-23.
An examination of policies and specific programmes for health in Slovenia, and the combined insurance scheme established in the 1970s. The influence of Slovenia's regional health policy on the other republics of Yugoslavia is also assessed.

310 **The epidemiology of venereal disease in Slovenia.**
   Janez Fettich. *European Journal of Sexually Transmitted Diseases*,
   vol. 3, no. 1 (1985), p. 35-6.
Although Slovenia has generally escaped the ravages of venereal diseases, including HIV/AIDS, its proximity to the port of Trieste and the number of international borders which Slovenia possesses, mean that the republic still faces some cases of venereal disease, particularly gonorrhea.

311 **The history of pyschology in former Yugoslavia – an overview.**
   K. Marinković. *Journal of the History of Behavioral Sciences*,
   vol. 28, no. 4 (1992), p. 340-51.
Marinković compares the provisions for psychological treatment in Slovenia with those in the other republics of the former Yugoslavia.

312 **Teaching medical ethics.**
   Janez Milčinski. *Journal of Medical Ethics*, vol. 6 (1980), p. 145-48.
Milčinski, a leading writer on medical/ethical problems explains what he believes to be good pedagogic practice when instructing junior doctors and nurses.

313 **Development of nursing in the northern part of Yugoslavia (S.R. of Slovenia).**
   P. Milena. *International Journal of Nursing Studies*, vol. 9, no. 3
   (1972), p. 151-8.
This brief history of nursing in Slovenia concentrates on the post-war period.

314 **The treatment of invasive carcinoma of the cervix at the department of gynaecology and obstetrics in Ljubljana.**
   Franc Novak. *European Journal of Gynaecological Oncology*, vol. 1,
   no. 1 (1980), p. 65-71.
Details of clinical practice regarding cervical cancer in Ljubljana hospitals.

315 **The optimality concept and its clinical value.**
   Milivoj Veliković Perat. *Early Human Development*, vol. 34, no. 1-2
   (Sept. 1993), p. 133-41.
All 124,759 newborn babies at 14 maternity hospitals in Slovenia from the period 1987 to 1991 were screened, to test Heinz F. R. Prechtl's original list of optimality. The present follow-up study has shown that predictions of disability were most accurate in the group of newborns who were clinically at risk at birth and who also had a low optimality score. The identification of these criteria 'is the best way to identify newborns who need special attention' (p. 133).

316   **Analysis of demand for private psychological practice (services) in Ljubljana.**
V. S. Rus, J. Susteršič.   *International Journal of Psychology*, vol. 27, no. 3-4 (1992), p. 622.

Abstract of a paper delivered at the 25th International Congress of Psychology in Brussels, 19-24 July 1992. Of related interest is *Alps-Adria Symposium of Psychology*. Edited by Janek Mušek and Marko Polič (Ljubljana: Bori, 1993. 309p.). It includes contributions by Slovenian authors.

317   **When the family does not function any more: the role of the community nurse in Slovenia.**
M. Slajmer-Japelj.   *Journal of Cross-Cultural Gerontology*, vol. 8, no. 4 (Oct. 1993), p. 325.

Slovenia still has a traditional and tight family network, although this has been partially eroded by population movements and other dislocation. This article discusses the role of nursing in this context.

Politics

318 **War in Slovenia.**
J. Avšar, translated by Dejan Šušnik, Liljana Živkovič.   Ljubljana:
Ljubljana International Press Center, 1991. 128p.

This documentary history of the conflict between the Slovenes and the Yugoslavian
People's Army in June and July 1991 includes some interesting pictures of the early
stages of the crisis of legitimacy of the Yugoslavian state in its northernmost republic.
For a personal account by one of the key players, the former Defence Minister Janez
Janša, see *The making of the Slovenian state 1988-1992: the collapse of Yugoslavia*
(Ljubljana: Mladinska knjiga, 1994. 251p.).

319 **Yugoslavia's bloody collapse: causes, course and consequences.**
Christopher Bennett.   London: Hurst, 1995. xv, 272p.

An account of the demise of Yugoslavia by a Slovene-speaking journalist, based in
London.

320 **The emergence of pluralism in Slovenia.**
Adolf Bibič.   *Communist and Post-Communist Studies*, vol. 26, no. 4
(Dec. 1993), p. 367-86.

An important article summarizing the factors that led to the political democratization
and ultimately to the independence of the Republic of Slovenia. Bibič emphasizes
three key factors: ideas about civil society (*civilna družba*), political pluralism and the
Slovenian National Question. Associations such as the Human Rights Committee or
the Slovenian Writers' Society and journals such as *Nova revija* are seen as being
particularly important to the development of ideas within society. The former
Communist élite can also be seen as important as they 'contributed decisively to
ensuring the relatively smooth and peaceful "velvet" transition of Slovenia to the
political pluralist system' (p. 373).

321 **Slovenia faces the future.**
Goražd Bohte. *Contemporary Review*, vol. 260, no. 5 (May 1992), p. 229-32.
An assessment of the political position of Slovenia after independence and international recognition, and a look at its place in a reconstructed Europe.

322 **The Yugoslav drama.**
Mihailo Črnobrnja. London: Tauris, 1994. xiv, 281p. maps.
This interesting account of the decline of Yugoslavia was written by one of its former ambassadors.

323 **Tito speaks: his self portrait and struggle with Stalin.**
Vladimir Dedijer. London: Weidenfeld and Nicholson, 1953. 456p.
No bibliography of Slovenian history and political culture would really be complete without some reference to the most famous of all South Slavs, himself half-Slovene. The literature on Tito is extensive, but Dedijer's assemblage is as good a place as any to start. For further reading see April Carter, *Marshal Tito: a bibliography* (Westport, Connecticut; London: Meckler, 1990. 150p.).

324 **Yugoslavia, Croatia, Slovenia: re-emerging boundaries.**
Greg Englefield. Durham: International Boundaries Research Unit Press, 1992. 54p. maps. (Territory Briefing, no. 3).
A study of the secessions of the republics of former Yugoslavia from a historical and territorial perspective. Englefield sees the former Yugoslavia as a 'zone of confrontation' (p. 2) between different religious faiths that still carries the legacy of the multi-national empires. He then surveys the international events up to June 1992, concluding that 'now that the Yugoslav project has failed, a new geo-political division of the region is developing based largely on crude nationalism and raw military strength, combined with political opportunism' (p. 136).

325 **Legitimacy and the military: the Yugoslav crisis.**
James Gow. London: Pinter, 1992. 204p.
Taking a long view of the crisis of legitimacy that accompanied the demise of Tito's Yugoslavia after the dictator's death, Gow's study focuses in particular on the role of civil–military relations. One of the flashpoints in the disintegration process was the scandal that erupted in July 1988 in Ljubljana that involved the trial of journalists (including the future defence minister, Janez Janša) who exposed military secrets to the press. Gow emphasizes the increasingly non-Slovene character of the army and the fact that the trial, conducted in secret and in Serbo-Croat, inflamed public opinion over the language issue and led, in turn, to a 'homogenisation of Slovene politics' in direct opposition to Belgrade centralism. See also his 'The deterioration of civil–military relations in Slovenia', *Slovo* (London), vol. 2, no. 1 (1989), p. 65-78.

326 **Slovenia – territorial defence a year on.**
James Gow. *Jane's Intelligence Review*, vol. 4, no. 7 (Aug. 1992), p. 305-08.
A review of post-independence defence arrangements by a leading authority on military matters.

327 **Political modernisation in Slovenia in the late 1980s and early 1990s.**
Danica Fink Hafner. *Journal of Communist Studies*, vol. 8, no. 4 (Dec. 1992), p. 210-26.

An analysis of Slovenia's transition from 'real socialism' to 'pluralist democracy', particularly focusing on the transformation of political culture and the role of new social movements. See also Hafner's *The transition of space of political inter-mediation and new patterns of policy making in Slovenia* (Budapest: Hungarian Center for Democracy Studies Foundation, 1922. 26p. [Budapest Papers on Democratic Transition, no. 26]).

328 **An evolution of the politics of fragmentation: a case study of Slovenes in Yugoslavia.**
A. Collins Jenko. Boston, Massachusetts: Boston University Press, 1984. 434p.

Looks at politics in Slovenia in the aftermath of the 1974 Constitution and the event of a more de-centralized political culture, and the place of Slovenes in the former Yugoslavia.

329 **Democracy and socialism.**
Edvard Kardelj, translated by Margot Milosavljević, Boško Milosavljević. London: Summerfield, 1978. 244p.

Edvard Kardelj, the most eminent post-war Slovene Communist was responsible for re-orientating Yugoslavian socialism after the break with Stalin in 1948. In this volume he discusses the main theoretical tenets of 'Yugoslavian socialism', including his views on self-management, on single-party systems and on democratic pluralism, and the development and changes in the self-managing society of Yugoslavia. The Belgrade-based Communist publishers, Socialist Thought and Practice, have also brought out *Socialism and war* (1979, 101p.); *Science and social criticism* (1980. 176p.); and *Self management and the political system* (1980. 287p.).

330 **Slovenia at the crossroads of the nineties: from the first multiparty elections and the declaration of independence to membership in the Council of Europe.**
Matjaž Klemenčič. *Slovene Studies*, vol. 14, no. 1 (1992), p. 9-34.

This detailed survey of the political developments from the late 1980s to a discussion of Slovenia's proposed associate membership of the EU and EFTA is particularly interesting in that he discusses the personalities behind the political parties and draws on quotations. He compares the elections of 1992 with the reconstruction period in the USA after the Civil War. (This point has been made in much more detail in his 'A letter to fellow Americanists', *Journal of American History*, vol. 80, no. 3 (Dec. 1993), p. 1031-4.)

331 **The Slovene spring.**
Miha Kovač, interviewed by Branka Magaš, Robin Blackburn. *New Left Review*, no. 171 (Sept.-Oct. 1988), p. 113-28.
This article is a useful summary of the political mood in Slovenia in 1988 and contains many prescient remarks about the growing problems within Yugoslavia. The former editor of the radical youth journal *Mladina* discusses the crisis of legitimacy within the League of Communists and the atmosphere of panic created by the arrest of journalists, including Janez Janša, and their subsequent military trial. Kovač argues that the roots of the democratization process can be traced back to the supression of the student movement and the liberal politicians in Slovenia in the early 1970s. The opposition are seen as belonging to camps, grouped around prominent publications such as the journals *Problemi*, which was influenced by French structuralism, and *Časopis za kritiko znanosti*, which was Marxist orientated. This so-called democratic opposition he places against the *Nova revija* group, which was the bastion of the traditional nationalist intelligentsia and the Slovene party itself. The Yugoslavian federation created nationalism through its political structures and Kovač argues that economic centralization combined with democratization are vital to 'socialist progress'.

332 **The destruction of Yugoslavia: tracking the breakup 1980-92.**
Branka Magaš. London: Verso, 1993. 366p.
This book is based on the journalistic writings of a leading left-winger and former editor of *New Left Review*, and comprises compelling accounts of the dissolution of Yugoslavia. Magaš combines an intimate knowledge of the major theoretical writings with a close acquaintance with individuals and organizations within the former Yugoslavia. The book includes an analysis of the growth of democracy in Slovenia. Of particular interest is her chapter 'Democracy and the National Question' (p. 137-55), written in September 1988 and addressing the problem of growing national awareness in Slovenia.

333 **Civil society in Slovenia.**
Tomaž Mastnak. In: *The tragedy of Yugoslavia – the failure of democratic transformation.* Edited by M. E. Sharpe. New York: Armonk, 1992, p. 49-66.
An article describing the emergence of a Slovenian political culture 'from below', looking in particular at the role of societies and the alternative arts scene.

334 **Slovenia: progress, problems and some squabbling.**
Patrick Moore, Stan Markotich. *Transition*, vol. 1, no. 1 (1995), p. 64-6. (Issues and Developments in the former Soviet Union and East-Central and Southeastern Europe).
Launched in 1995 by the Open Media Research Institute in Prague, *Transition* promises to be an interesting forum for the presentation of up-to-the-minute information about the political situations in the former Communist countries in Eastern Europe. This article considers the problems that the Alpine Republic has faced during 1994, including tense relations with Italy and Croatia, and the 'Smolnikar Affair', which led to the resignation of Defence Minister Janez Janša.

335 **Secessionist self-determination: the cases of Slovenia and Croatia.**
Peter Radan. *Australian Journal of International Affairs*, vol. 48,
no. 2 (Nov. 1994), p. 183-96.
Assesses the international position of Slovenia and Croatia after independence.

336 **'Slovenia will become an independent state': an interview with
Dimitrij Rupel.**
Pedro Ramet. *South Slav Journal*, vol. 12, nos. 1-2 (Spring-Summer
1989), p. 81-6.
One of the founders of the Democratic Union (DEMOS) talks about the political
climate in Slovenia the year before secession, and about the prospects for Yugoslavia.
Rupel seemed to believe that the choices at this stage were either a 'proper
confederation' or a 'sovereign (i.e. independent) state', backing his claims by
referring to public opinion about the economic situation of the Slovenes within
Yugoslavia.

337 **Nationalism and federalism in Yugoslavia 1962-1991.**
Sabrina P. Ramet.   Bloomington and Indianapolis: Indiana University
Press, 1992. xviii, 346p.
An empirically detailed account of the links between the different Yugoslavian
republics since 1962, including an analysis of the so-called 'Kavčič Affair', when the
then President, Stane Kavčič, was forced to resign after objecting to Belgrade's
acquisition of money destined for a road-building project in Slovenia. This is a useful
source of information for all the republics, which tends to stress the autonomy of
nationalist currents as opposed to other narratives which have given weight to Serbian
nationalism. As ever, Ramet has consulted a great deal of primary material including
the Slovenian newpapers *Delo* and *Dnevnik*. For a Slovene perspective on the
disintegration of Yugoslavia, see Anton Bebler, 'Yugoslavia's variety of Communist
federalism and her demise', *Communist and Post-Communist Studies*, vol. 26, no. 1
(March 1993), p. 72-86.

338 **Slovenia's road to democracy.**
Sabrina P. Ramet. *Europe-Asia Studies*, vol. 45, no. 5 (1993),
p. 869-86.
Utilizing material drawn from newspaper articles and radio broadcasts as well as
personal interviews with leading Slovenians – including Lojže Peterle in March 1992
– Ramet surveys Slovenian political, social and economic developments between 1986
and 1992. Moves towards independence are seen largely as a culmination of
oppositional trends since Milan Kučan became 'de facto arbiter of Slovenian political
life'. After discussing the diplomatic and military struggle to achieve independence,
she moves on to examine the 'pressing tasks' facing the new republic. She recognizes
the 'democratic achievements of the Slovenians and is optimistic about longer-term
prospects for economic development, but nevertheless recognizes that problems –
such as unemployment, a sluggish transition to full privatization and caring for
Bosnian refugees – will dog the republic in the short term.

339 **The education of a Slovene Marxist: Edvard Kardelj 1924-34.**
Carole Rogel. *Slovene Studies*, vol. 11, nos. 1-2 (1989), p. 177-84.
Rogel examines Edvard Kardelj's political education, including his time in prison, and his views on fascism as it was emerging in Central and Eastern Europe.

340 **Post mortem – elections in Slovenia on December 6, 1992.**
Ljubo Sirc. *South Slav Journal*, vol. 14, nos. 1-2 (Spring-Summer 1991, printed 1993), p. 43-52.
This pessimistic consideration of the continuity in power of the Slovenian 'Communists', was written by a failed candidate for the Presidency.

341 **Red Adriatic: the Communist parties of Italy and Yugoslavia.**
Eric R. Terzuolo. Boulder, Colorado: Westview, 1985. 255p. bibliog.
In his comparison of two Mediterranean Communist parties, the Yugoslavian and the Italian, Terzuolo discusses the regional variations within the party, the role of nationalism and border disputes after the Second World War.

342 **Slovenia between liberalisation and democratisation.**
Cyril A. Žebot. *Slovene Studies*, vol. 11, nos. 1-2 (1989), p. 231-43.
An overview of political developments in Slovenia in the 1980s, in whch Žebot compares it to *glasnost* in the Soviet Union.

343 **The Slovenes' first rejection of Yugoslavia.**
Momcilo Zečević. *South Slav Journal*, vol. 15, nos. 3-4 (Autumn-Winter 1994), p. 2-10.
Zečević's polemical account of the break-up of Yugoslavia, written with extreme antipathy to Slovenian nationalism, aims to answer the question 'how could a people with such a pronounced commitment to Yugoslavia and to statehood, which the Slovenes undoubtedly had been since 1918, find themselves in the role of the main wrecker of Yugoslavia?'

The Constitution and Legal System

344 **Constitution of the Republic of Slovenia.**
Edited by Miro Čerar, Janez Kranjc, translated by Sherill O'Connor,
Pavel Sranj, Garry Moore.   Ljubljana: Časopisni zavod uradni list
Republike Slovenije, 1993. 79p.
A clear English transation of the Slovenian Constitution promulgated in 1991, which
replaced the Yugoslavian Constitution of 1974.

345 **The genesis of the contractual theory and the installation of the
Dukes of Carinthia.**
Joseph Felicjan.   Klagenfurt, Austria: Družba svetega Mohorja, 1967.
144p.
Outlines the history of the ceremony that took place at Gospa sveta in the Middle
Ages, in which the Dukes of Carinthia were installed (*ustoličevanje*) on a stone
(*knežni kamen*). Felicjan conjectures about the relationship between this ceremony
and other democratic procedures, thus linking Jean Bodin and Thomas Jefferson to the
Carinthian Slovenes.

346 **The evolving legal framework for private sector activity in
Slovenia.**
C. W. Gray, F. D. Stiblar.   *University of Pennsylvania Journal of
International Business Law*, vol. 14, no. 2 (1993), p. 119-67.
Outlines the legal constraints for private enterprise and the changes in the laws since
1990. See also C. W. Williams, *The evolving legal framework for private sector
activity in Slovenia* (Washington, DC: Socialist Economies Reform Unit, Country
Economics Dept, World Bank, 1992. 34p.).

347 **Public trust in the new parliaments of Central and Eastern Europe.**
J. R. Hibbing, S. C. Patterson. *Political Studies*, vol. 42, no. 4 (1994), p. 570-92.

Assesses public opinion surveys in nine countries (including Slovenia) in 1990-91. In Slovenia, the preliminary results suggest approximately 50 per cent of the population have little or no trust in their Parliament. As the authors point out, 'the timing of multi-party elections in Slovenia was such that survey respondents must have been appraising the tricameral parliament still existing at the end of Slovenia's tenure as a constituent member of the Socialist Federal Republic of Yugoslavia' (p. 576). Analysts of politics will therefore have to seek more conclusive evidence about political opinion in the Alpine republic.

348 **Cohabitation without marriage: the Yugoslav experience.**
Petar Sarčević. *American Journal of Comparative Law*, vol. 29, no. 2 (Spring 1981), p. 315-38.

In the former Yugoslavia, only in Slovenia were cohabitations considered by republican law to be equal to marital relationships. This difference from the other republics had consequences for inter-republican relationships and questions of the legitimacy of children.

349 **Law on commercial companies.**
Slovenian Business Report, no. 7-8 (July-Aug. 1993), p. 13-60.

A full English translation of the 596 articles governing commercial companies in the Republic of Slovenia, as ratified by the National Assembly on 27 May 1993.

350 **Important legislation in the Republic of Slovenia.**
Slovenian Business Report, no. 11 (Nov. 1993), p. 34-5.

A summary of the contents of the weekly *Uradni list Republike Slovenije* (*Official Gazette of the Republic of Slovenia*) relating to foreign trade, customs, internal trade, the commercial sector, foreign investment, the monetary system, banking and international agreements.

Administration and Local Government

351 **The impact of national, political and economic structures on local government: an international comparison of four cities (Niigata, Japan; Olsztyn, Poland; Ljubljana, Slovenia; Richmond, Virginia).**
Henry V. Harman.   PhD, Virginia Commonwealth University, 1993.
182p.

Examines whether economic and political structures of nations affect local government. Ljubljana was chosen as a case-study because it contrasts with the other terms of its level of national economic planning and decentralization. See also Mark J. Kassoff, 'Local government in Yugoslavia and the constitutional reform of 1974: a case study of Ljubljana', *Journal of the American Institute of Planners,* vol. 42, no. 4 (Oct. 1976), p. 399-409, which examines the way in Ljubljana's citizens responded to changes in local government after 1974, with particular reference to the city's transport network and to the role of self-management.

Foreign Relations

352 **Slovenia and Europe.**
Anton Bebler. *The World Today* (The Royal Institute of International Affairs), vol. 51, no. 5 (May 1995), p. 96-9.
An international perspective on Slovenian politics, which concentrates on problematic bilateral relations with the Italians and the Croatians as well as examining Slovenia's position within the wider European community. See also Bebler's 'The Republic of Slovenia', *Perspectives* (Prague), no. 4 (Winter 1994/95), p. 25-33.

353 **The international community and the case of Croatia and Slovenia.**
N. S. Dokič. *International Spectator*, vol. 27, no. 4 (Oct.-Dec. 1992), p. 81-94.
Analyses the reponse of the international community, particularly Britain, France, Germany and the United States to Slovenian and Croatian declarations of independence in 1991 and the lengthy period before full recognition was achieved.

354 **The case of Slovenia.**
Edited by Niko Grafenauer. Ljubljana: Nova revija, 1991. 228p.
Written in the immediate circumstances of the invasion of Slovenia by the Yugoslavian People's Army in the summer of 1991, this illustrated book is an emotional plea for Slovenian independence to be acknowledged by the rest of the world.

355 **U.S. policy towards the demise of Yugoslavia: the 'virus of nationalism'.**
Paula Franklin Lytle. *East European Politics and Societies*, vol. 6, no. 3 (Fall 1992), p. 303-18.
A linguistic deconstruction of the US policy statements about former Yugoslavia, particularly Slovenia and Croatia, in which Lytle points out that nationalism is often equated with a disease or illness. The political consequence of this, she argues, has

been to equate Slovenian or Croatian nationalism with Serbian, and a failure to understand the function of nationalist discourse in a post-Communist society.

356 Historical constraints in political, social and economic cooperation in the Alpe-Adria area.
Andreas Moritsch. *Slovene Studies*, vol. 10, no. 1 (1988), p. 9-14.

Attempts to foster cooperation between the different countries of the Eastern Alps have existed since the 1960s. The earthquake in Friuli in 1976 led to increased moves for intra-regional cooperation and the Alpe-Adria Working Community was set up in 1978. Its core regions were initially Carinthia and Styria in Austria, Slovenia in Yugoslavia and Friuli-Venezia-Giulia in Italy, although other regions have subsequently joined. Moritsch, a leading Austrian historian, argues that this movement has strong historical precedents, tracing his argument back to the Middle Ages. By the seventeenth century, the Habsburg province of Inner Austria had become 'a virtually independent state', and in the nineteenth century Archduke Johann founded an economic organization to help local trade and industry. It was 'rising nationalism' that acted as a centrifugal force in this region, dividing peoples of a 'similar outlook'. The ghosts of nationalism, according to Moritsch remain to be exploited by 'political adventurers', ultimately hindering the recreation of a supranational Central European identity. In a reply to Moritsch in the same volume of *Slovene Studies* entitled 'Commentary: the historical background of Alpe-Adria cooperation' (p. 15-19), Peter Vodopivec argues that 'the failure of the Yugoslavians to find a really effective modus vivendi' can in part be attributed to the way in which nineteenth-century nationalisms shattered an older regional identity in the Alpe-Adria region.

357 Slovenia – sovereignty aimed at integration.
Lojže Peterle. *Studia Diplomatica*, vol. 47, no. 5 (1994), p. 3-7.

A discussion of Slovenia's political position in Europe by the former Prime Minister and prominent Christian Democrat politician.

358 'Friendly concern': Europe's decision-making on the recognition of Slovenia and Croatia.
Hans-Heinrich Wrede. *Oxford International Review*, vol. 4 (Spring 1993), p. 30-2.

Analyses the policy statements and political objectives of the major Western European powers over the independence of Slovenia and Croatia.

Economy

General

359 Slovenian lands and their economies, 1848-1873.
John A. Arnez. New York: Studia Slovenica, 1983. 321p. map.
Examines the growth of the agricultural and industrial sectors of the economy after the end of feudal restrictions in 1848, but before the Stock Exchange crash in Vienna in 1873. Arnez covers the nine administrative units where Slovenes lived within the Habsburg monarchy.

360 The economic thought of Dr. Janez Evangelist Krek.
John A. Arnez. *Slovene Studies*, vol. 11, nos. 1-2 (1989), p. 65-74.
Krek (1865-1917), theology professor and representative in the Viennese Parliament, was particularly interested in worker and peasant education. He formulated a Christian anti-capitalist economic doctrine and was critical of the role of money in society. See also B. Černič, 'The role of Dr. Janez Evangelist Krek in the Slovene cooperative movement', *Slovene Studies*, vol. 11, nos. 1-2 (1989), p. 75-81.

361 Co-operative movements in Eastern Europe: Czechoslovakia, Yugoslavia, Poland.
Edited by Aloysius Balawyder. New York, London: Macmillan, 1980. 211p.
Includes three articles on Slovenia: 'The co-operative movement in Slovenia', by Rudolf Čuješ (p. 83-109); 'The private sector in the economy of the Socialist Republic of Slovenia', by Ciril A. Žebot (p. 111-47), accompanied by a discussion by Toussaint Hočevar (p. 149-52).

362 **Worker's cooperatives – a means to humanise the economy.**
Rudolf Čuješ. *Slovene Studies*, vol. 11, nos. 1-2 (1989), p. 119-25.
A brief history of cooperativism, looking particularly at the work of the Slovene philosopher France Verber. See also Rudolf P. Čuješ, *Slovenia: land of co-operators* (Willowdale, Ontario: Slovenian Research Centre, 1985. 66p.), and W. Lukan, 'The second phase of Slovene cooperativism (1894-1918)', *Slovene Studies*, vol. 11, nos. 1-2 (1989), p. 83-95.

363 **The economic rise of the Habsburg Empire 1750-1914.**
David F. Good. Berkeley: University of California Press, 1984. xvi, 309p.
The standard text on the economic history of the Habsburg monarchy during its last 164 years. This book is of particular use to students of Slovene history in that it covers the growth of the port of Trieste.

364 **Economic issues underlying secession – the case of Slovenia and Slovakia.**
Milica Žarković-Bookman. *Communist Economies and Economic Transformation*, vol. 4, no. 1 (1992), p. 111-34.
Compares the economics of secession in two federations of Eastern Europe: Yugoslavia and Czechoslovakia. Slovenia is more ethnically homogeneous, has a slightly higher income per capita and is more industrialized than Slovakia, but both share the influence of the Catholic Church. The author adopts several criteria, including levels of income and trade to assess the viability of the economies, and concludes that 'the number of economic questions that must be resolved is almost endless' (p. 127).

Regional and local

365 **Transition in Eastern Europe.**
Edited by Olivier Blanchard, Kenneth Froot, Jeffrey Sachs. Chicago: University of Chicago Press, 1994. 2 vols.
An assessment of the practical and theoretical problems facing Eastern Europe since 1989, including an article on political independence and economic reform in Slovenia by Boris Pleškovič and Jeffrey Sachs.

366 **Recent trends in economic cooperation and development in the Alpe-Adria region.**
Giacomo Borusso, Romeo Danielis. *Slovene Studies*, vol. 10, no. 1 (1988), p. 21-5.
Reviews the Alpe-Adria as an economic region with a developing network of cooperation.

367 **Costs and benefits of independence – Slovenia.**
M. Cvikl, M. Vodopivec, E. Kraft. *Communist Economies and Economic Transformation*, vol. 5, no. 3 (1993), p. 295-315.

Debates the consequences for Slovenia of lost markets in Southeastern Europe and opportunities to spread into Central Europe. Argues that Slovenia is essentially different from other parts of the former Yugoslavia, or indeed the former Czechoslovakia, and although a far greater economic autonomy is possible now, in the long term Slovenia would benefit from economic cooperation with its former Yugoslavian partners.

368 **Bosnia-Hercegovina, Croatia, Slovenia.**
Economic Intelligence Unit. London: E.I.U., 1995. 62p. maps. (Country Profile, 1994-5).

Statistical information on Slovenia's political and financial fortunes, including the population of towns, political parties, as well as GDP by sectoral origin, agricultural and trade figures. The E. I. U. format is highly accessible because of the clear charts. Much of the information has come directly from the statistical office of the Republic of Slovenia.

369 **The structure of the Slovenian economy: 1848-1963.**
Toussaint Hočevar. New York: Studia Slovenica, 1965. 277p. bibliog.

Covers the economic history of the Slovene lands from the end of the feudal era to the establishment of the Titoist economic system, which included self-management, increased industrialization and agricultural cooperatives. See also Hočevar's *Slovenia's role in the Yugoslav economy* (Columbus, Ohio: Slovenian Research Center, 1964. 64p.) and his 'Equilibrium in linguistic minority markets', *Kyklos*, vol. 28, no. 2 (1975), p. 337-57.

370 **Financial intermediation in a multilingual state: the case of Slovene corporate banking in Austria, 1900-12.**
Toussaint Hočevar. *Slovene Studies*, vol. 8, no. 1 (1986), p. 45-56.

Examines the link between finance and national or ethnic self-consciousness in the twilight years of the Habsburg monarchy.

371 **Input–output relationships in the Slovene economy in 1986.**
I. Lavrac. *Slovene Studies*, vol. 11, nos. 1-2 (1989), p. 109-17.

Argues that a grid called an input–output table is one of the most effective ways of portraying an economy, giving a 'holistic' view of the Slovene economy in 1986.

372 **Slovene economy in the eighties.**
Edited by Warren F. Mazek. New York: Society for Slovene Studies, 1981. 49p.

A special edition of two papers: 'The role of the agricultural sector in the Slovene economy' by Frank Oražem and 'Structural transformation in the economy of Slovenia', by the well-known American-Slovene economist Toussaint Hočevar (1927-87).

373 **Contrasts in emerging societies: readings in the social and economic history of South-eastern Europe in the nineteenth century.**
Edited by Doreen Warriner. London: Athlone Press, 1965. 402p. maps.

An extremely useful text in that it presents several 'classic' articles about Slovenia in English, including Janez Bleiweiss on 'The need for agricultural progress' (p. 355-8), Balthasar Hacquet on 'The margins of existence' (p. 349-53) and Gustav Pirc on 'The causes of agricultual depression (1893)' (p. 361-3).

374 **The economic consequences of national independence – the case of Slovenia.**
Kenneth Zapp. *International Journal of Politics, Culture and Society*, vol. 7, no. 1 (Fall 1993), p. 57-74.

After assessing the historical causes of Slovenia's independence, Zapp considers the challenges for the Slovenian economy in the context of lost markets in the former Yugoslavia and unease about privatization. This is a useful examination of the transition period.

375 **The economic basis of regional autarchy in Yugoslavia.**
Milica Žarković-Bookman. *Soviet Studies*, vol. 42, no. 1 (Jan. 1990), p. 93-109.

Compares the economics of the Republic of Slovenia and the region of Vojvodina. See also her *Economic decline and nationalism in the Balkans* (New York: St Martin's Press, 1994. 214p.).

376 **Slovenia – one year of independence.**
Egon Žižmond. *Europe-Asia Studies*, vol. 45, no. 5 (1993), p. 869-86.

A summary of the state of the economy in Slovenia, by one of its leading experts. See also his 'Levels and disparities of retail prices in Slovenia', *Revista Internazionale di Scienze Economiche e Commerciali* (Milan), vol. 39, nos. 5-6 (1993), p. 521.

Finance and Banking

377 **Privatisation in Eastern Europe: current implementation issues
with a collection of privatisation laws.**
Edited by Andreja Boehm, Vladimir G. Kreačič. Ljubljana:
International Center for Public Enterprises in Developing Countries
(ICPE Publications), 1991. 187p.

Before the demise of Yugoslavia, the ICPE was chiefly a source for literature relating
to development economics. In this book they have published legal documents relating
to privatization in Eastern Europe as well as presenting a discussion of the Slovenian
case written by Marko Simoneti and Uros Korže, in which they argue that
privatization was highly centralized but also closely regulated. Of related interest is
Privatisation: an International Symposium (London: London Centre for Research into
Communist Economics, 1992. 132p.).

378 **Monetary reform: the case of Slovenia.**
Sasha Chetkovich, Sven Chetkovich. Stockholm: Stockholm Institute
of Soviet and East European Economics: Oestekonomiska Institutet,
1992. 36p. (Working Papers, no. 44).

Considers the challenges associated with the creation of the Slovenian *tolar*, its
international status as a currency and the problems of transition from the Yugoslavian
dinar.

379 **Decentralisation privatisation: the Slovene ESOP program.**
David P. Ellerman, Uros Korže, Marko Simoneti. *Public Enterprise*,
vol. 11, nos. 2-3 (1991), p. 175-84.

Looks at the initial privatization programme and the Employee Stock Ownership Plan
(ESOP) both in Slovenia and internationally up to 1991. Of related interest is Jože
Mencinger, *Decentralised versus centralised privatisation: the case of Slovenia*
(Chapel Hill, North Carolina: Kenan Flager Business School, 1992). Mencinger is also
the author of *The Yugoslav economy: systematic changes 1945-86* (Pittsburgh:
University of Pittsburgh Center for Russian and East European Studies, 1989. 33p.).

380 **Reflections on the 'Gruenderboom' and the Stock Exchange crash of 1873 among the Slovenes.**
Stane Granda. *Slovene Studies*, vol. 11, nos. 1-2 (1989), p. 33-46.
Granda assesses the effect of rapid industrialization in the 1860s and 1870s and the subsequent development of a Slovenian economy.

381 **Slovenia: a new state and its prospects.**
Jože Mencinger. In: *Eastern Europe in crisis and the way out.* Edited by Christopher T. Saunders. London: Macmillan (in association with the Vienna Institute for Comparative Economic Studies), 1955, p. 472-89. (European Economic Integration Workshop papers, vol. 15).
Compares the political 'success story' of Slovenian independence with the less spectacular achievements in the economic sphere, including stabilization with contraction and disappointing privatization. The work includes a statistical appendix of Slovenian foreign trade 1992-93 and a regional structure of trade within Slovenia 1991-93.

382 **How to create a currency – the experience of Slovenia.**
Jože Mencinger. *Review of World Economics*, vol. 129, no. 2 (1993), p. 418-31.
Looks at the events and problems surrounding the creation of the Slovenian *tolar* and attempts to sustain its value within the international currency market.

383 **Money and finance in Yugoslavia.**
Ivan Ribnikar. *Slovene Studies*, vol. 11, nos. 1-2 (1989), p. 223-30.
Looks at the financial system in Yugoslavia in its final years, including attempted reforms, the availability of credit, inflation, and the international position of the *dinar*.

384 **Foreign investment in Slovenia – experience, prospects and policy options.**
M. Rojec, M. Svetličič. *Communist Economies and Economic Transformation*, vol. 5, no. 1 (1993), p. 103-14.
Outlines the problems that face foreign investors in Slovenia and the opportunities for expansion.

385   **Privatisation and economic reform in Central Europe: the
       changing business climate.**
       Edited by Dennis A. Rondivelli.   Westport, Connecticut: Quorum
       Books, 1994. 288p.

A collection of essays, which includes the following contributions on Slovenia: in
'Decentralisation of administrative and political authority to promote regional
economic development: the case of Ljubljana' (p. 107-21), Pavel Ganthar assesses a
study by the Ljubljana Regional Chamber of Economy; in 'Decentralisation versus
centralised privatisation: the case of Slovenia' (p. 93-105), Jože Mencinger looks at
some of the dilemmas that a transformation from a socialist to a market economy
brings; while in 'Privatisation of Tobacco Company Ljubljana' (p. 123-34), Uroš
Korže and Marko Simoneti argue that general lessons can be learnt from a trade sales
case.

Trade and Industry

386 Can trade losses explain the current recession in Slovenia?
Timothy Stephen Buehrer. PhD, Harvard University, 1994. 165p.
Since 1990 and the first economic moves to secede from Yugoslavia, Slovenia's GDP
has dropped by 16 per cent and Eastern European trade has declined dramatically.
Buehrer argues that although trade loss can probably account for two-thirds of this
decline, other reasons for decline, such as changes in the structure of the economy,
must be considered.

387 Nuclear power plant Krško.
Milan Čopič. Krško, Slovenia: Nuclear Power Plant, 1987. 23p.
The plant at Krško has proved to be a bone of contention in Slovenian politics, both
from the environmental lobby and recently concerning bilateral relations with the
Republic of Croatia. Here Čopič outlines the plant's history and its operations.

**388 The Slovene labourer and his experience of industrialisation
1888-1976.**
James C. Davis. *East European Quarterly*, vol. 10, no. 1 (1976),
p. 3-10.
This article is based on the life of the author's father-in-law, Franz Žužek, who was
born in 1888 in a village in the Triestine Karst. His life history reflects the slow
process of industrialization in this area, in that most of the changes associated with
modernization occurred during his lifetime. These changes are seen as, for example, a
rise in living standards, the emergence of new towns, the selling off of agricultural
land by farmers; decline in family size; the destruction of the landscape through ugly
buildings; and the use of *ti* (you-informal) instead of *vi* (you-formal). 'As for religion,
only the old and some women and little children go on Sundays to the little churches
in Sistiana and Malchina' (p. 18).

389 **The population in handicrafts and industry in Slovenia from the mid-nineteenth century until the First World War.**
Jasna Fischer. *Slovene Studies*, vol. 11, nos. 1-2 (1989), p. 47-56.

Fischer looks at material from five censuses taken between 1869 and 1910, and then uses this to investigate the distribution of handicrafts and other light industries, and the numbers of people involved in these.

390 **Agreement between the member states of the European Coal and Steel Community and the European Coal and Steel Community of the one part and the Republic of Slovenia, of the other part with final act and declarations, Luxembourg, 5 April, 1993.**
H.M.S.O. Luxembourg: European Communities, 3 (1994). 29p. (1992 Series).

Official documentation relating to the trade between Slovenia and the EU. Of related interest is B. Pečenko, 'Franchising in Slovenia', *Public Enterprise*, no. 1-2 (March-June 1993), p. 33.

391 **Changes in the hierachy of motivational factors and social values in Slovenian industry.**
Misha D. Jezernik. *Journal of Social Issues*, vol. 24, no. 2 (April 1968), p. 103-11.

Looks at some of the problems within Slovene industry in the context of self-management and other worker participation.

392 **A lead-zinc enterprise in Yugoslavia.**
Charles W. Loch. *Mining Magazine* (London), vol. 56, no. 4 (Oct. 1939), p. 201-15.

Mines have existed in Mežica in Slovenian Carinthia since the mid-eighteenth century. This article, written at a time when the mine-owners were Central European Mines Ltd, outlines the history, geological structure and ore-bodies, as well as giving plans of individual mines and detailing the industrial and trading characteristics of the enterprise. Of related interest is Boris Berce, 'The formation of ore deposits in Slovenia', *Rendicondi della Società Mineralogica Italiana*, vol. 19 (1963), p. 1-16.

393 **The design quality of products: a method of pursuing innovation.**
A. Lokar. *Slovene Studies*, vol. 11, nos. 1-2 (1989), p. 127-36.

Lokar, a Slovene economist based in Udine, discusses the role of innovation in economic theory, particularly with regard to the ideas of Joseph Schumpeter. He uses examples from his own research.

394 **A Yugoslav new town.**
Saša Sedlar. *Town and Country Planning*, vol. 29, no. 3 (March 1961), p. 111-14.

Describes the post-war development of the coal town Velenje (Titovo Velenje), whose experimental architecture represented Yugoslavian town design at both its best and its worst.

Agriculture and Forestry

395 The role of landscape ecology in forestry.
Edited by Boštjan Anko.   Ljubljana: Biotechnical Faculty,
Department of Forestry, 1993. 131p.

Proceedings of the IUFRO Working Party, held in Slovenia in September 1993. See
also Milan Šinko, *Forest and forest products country profile/Slovenia* (New York:
United Nations, 1994. 34p. [Geneva Timber and Forest Study Papers, no. 2]).

396 Agricultural cooperatives in the Republic of Slovenia.
F. Avsec.   *Review of International Cooperation*, vol. 87, no. 2 (1994),
p. 78-83.

Avsec assesses the state of agricultural cooperatives in the context of the decline of
the socialist economy.

**397 The family of foresters and sawyers in the southern Pohorje during
the period of the capitalist exploitation of the forests.**
Angelos Baš.   *Etnologia Slavica*, vol. 8/9 (1976-77), p. 217-26.

Describes the social patterns and practices of the foresters and sawyers of the Pohorje
region (between Maribor and Dravograd). From about 1900, there were about 40
foresters and their families living on estates belonging to noble families, who led
essentially separate lives from the peasantry and had their own social norms. These
norms are described here, including details about leisure, marriage, child-rearing and
old age.

398   **On the typology and regional spatial transformation of the viticultural country in the Socialist Republic of Slovenia (Yugoslavia).**
Borut Belec.   In: *Agricultural typology and land utilisation.*   Verona, Italy: Università di Verona, Centro di Geografia Agricola, 1975, p. 41-53.

Slovenia has a long tradition of wine growing and has several distinct wine regions, including the Eastern region of Haloze, where Haložan is produced, and the Karst area near Trieste which specializes in wines such as Rebula. Slovenians use both native grapes and imports such as *beli pinot* in their viticulture. This article looks at the wine industry and the economic changes since the Second World War that have led to an increase in production.

399   **The process of individualisation of agriculture in Carniola in the second half of the nineteenth century.**
Marjan Britovšek.   *East European Quarterly*, vol. 3, no. 4 (Jan. 1970), p. 469-88.

Britovšek looks at the impact of the feudal agrarian structure in Carniola (Kranjska) after 1848.

400   **Problems of socialist policy in the countryside.**
Edvard Kardelj, translated by Sonia Bičanić.   London: Lincolns-Prager, 1962. 304p.

After the break with Stalin in 1948, the Yugoslavians were obliged to seek different approaches to creating a socialist economy, particularly a solution to the land question which was acceptable to the peasantry. While still holding the collective farm as the socialist ideal, Kardelj discusses the economics of transition in the countryside. For a critique of Kardelj's economics by a leading Slovene former dissident, see Ljubo Sirc, *The Yugoslav economy under self-management* (London: Macmillan, 1979. 270p.).

401   **Agriculture under socialism.**
Frank Oražem.   *Slovene Studies*, vol. 11, nos. 1-2 (1989), p. 215-22.

Oražem assesses agriculture under Communist regimes, turning specifically to Slovenia, and outlines agricultural developments in the republic from 1945 onwards; by the 1980s state agriculture accounted for 56 per cent of the total. See also Theodore Buila, 'Agricultural education in Yugoslavia' (PhD dissertation, Cornell University, 1968. 305p.).

402   **Contemporary changes in the agricultural use of land in the border landscape units of the Slovene littoral.**
Branko Pavlin, Bruce Peterson.   Ljubljana: Inštitut za geografijo, Univerza v Ljubljani, 1991. 124p. maps.

The Slovene littoral can in some respects be characterized as typically Mediterranean, with land given over to the cultivation of olives, vines and fruit. It also shares some inland characteristics, in that pig and dairy farming are also widespread. This illustrated study assesses the relative changes that have occurred in the last few years to the agricultural landscape.

403 **Efficiency and ownership in Slovene dairying.**
Jennifer Piesse, C. Thirtle, Jernej Turk.   Reading, England: University of Reading, Dept of Economics, [n.d.]. 37p. (Series G, vol. 1, no. 2).

An occasional paper produced by a research team based both in Reading and Ljubljana, which examines recent improvements and legal changes with regard to the important dairy industry in Slovenia.

404 **Agrarian economy in Slovenia.**
I. Vriser.   *Geojournal*, vol. 31, no. 4 (Dec. 1993), p. 373-8.

A general survey of agriculture in Slovenia, in the context of recent changes to that section of the economy.

Transport

405 The transport system of of Slovenia – problems and perspectives.
M. Janić.   *Transport Reviews*, vol. 148, no. 3 (1994), p. 269-85.

Slovenia's transport system has both gained and suffered since independence in 1991. Public transport is still predominantly in the form of frequent bus and coach services and a rail service links most of the large towns to neighbouring countries, although journeys are in some cases slow and complex. Road users still face delays on the Alpine passes and Slovenia also suffers the continuous presence of road traffic from Western and Central Europe to Southern destinations. See also Bogdan Zgonc, 'Slovenian railways', *Rail International*, vol. 23, no. 12 (Dec. 1992), p. 26-31.

406 The development of the Yugoslav railways and their gravitation toward Trieste.
Anton Melik.   Belgrade: Yugoslavian Government Publications, 1945. 15p. maps.

An officially sponsored and polemical pamphlet, charting the growth of railways in the former Yugoslavia, and particularly Slovenia, since 1846.   Melik's overall aim was to 'prove' that Trieste was integrated into the economy of its hinterland in order to bolster the communists' claims to the Adriatic port after the Second World War. The text is in Russian, French and English. For a more detailed study of Trieste and its railways, see Andreas Moritsch, 'Der Niedergang des Fuhrwerkswesens nach der Errichtung der Eisenbahnen am Beispiel einiger Verkehrshilforte im Slovenischen Kuestenland (Slovensko primorje)', (The decline in the use of carts following the building of railways, with evidence from several relief stations on the Slovenian coast) *East European Quarterly*, vol. 3, no. 4 (Jan. 1970), p. 489-98.

407 The Karawanken tunnel: gateway to Yugoslavia.
Tone Vahen.   *Yugoslav Review*, no. 5/6 (1987), p. 24-5.

The Karawanken tunnel project described here made road and rail acceses between Slovenia and Austria immeasurably easier and lightened the burden on existing routes.

Employment, Labour and Manpower

408 **The real wage/employment relationship and employment in transitional economies: the case of Slovenia and Hungary.**
Alenka Kajzer. Budapest: Institute for World Economics, Hungarian Academy of Sciences, 1994. 31p.
A working paper comparing post-Communist economic development in Hungary and Slovenia, suggesting that worker expectations, in terms of wages, are too high and that this in turn results in higher unemployment.

409 **Human resource management during the restructuring of the Jesenice Iron and Steel Works.**
Iztok Kremšer, Tomaž Ramuš, Ales Vahčič. *Public Enterprise*, vol. 9, no. 2 (1989), p. 221-8.
Steel and iron works have existed in Jesenice since 1869 and the technology of production has changed vastly during that time. The article outlines the attempts to retrain employees during the 1980s, given a reduction in overall staffing.

410 **A success story: modern management producing productivity in a plant in a less developed area of Slovenia.**
R. Palčič, M. Mulej. *Public Enterprise*, vol. 14, no. 1-2 (1994), p. 121-31.
Looks at attempts to introduce new management techniques in Eastern Slovenia.

411 **Women entrepreneurs in Slovenia.**
M. Turk. *Public Enterprise*, vol. 12, no. 1-2 (1992), p. 126-34.
Since 1990, due to deregulation in the economy, the number of women entrepreneurs has grown, particularly those owning franchises of large foreign companies in the fashion, cosmetic and restaurant industries.

Statistics

412 **Slovenija. Predpisi: standardna klasifikacija dejavnosti.** (Slovenia.
Regulations: standard classification of activities.)
Edited by Alenka Leskovič.   Ljubljana: Uradni list Republike
Slovenije, 1994. 96p.
Comprehensive list of statistics relating to business activities, published in Slovene.
The best statistical sources of information in English are to be found in the weekly *IN:
Information from Slovenia* (see item no. 586).

413 **Statistični letopis Slovenije.**
Ljubljana: Zavod Slovenije za statistiko. annual.
Annual digest of statistical information on public health, justice and demography,
collated from governmental sources for the country as a whole or broken down by
občina (the unit of local government).

Environment

Town planning

414 Planning and management of water resources in the Ljubljana region of Yugoslavia.
Thomas R. Angotti. *Environmental Conservation*, vol. 3, no. 3 (Autumn 1976), p. 189-95.
Looks at water and waste management in Ljubljana, in the context of the Slovenians' particular concern for environmental care and cost.

415 Planning and housing in the Yugoslav Republic of Slovenia.
Daniel R. Mandelker. *Urban Law and Policy*, vol. 4, no. 4 (1981), p. 357-72.
Mandelker describes the social planning of housing and the Slovenian concern for citizen participation.

416 New housing challenges in Slovenia.
S. Mandič, T. Rop. *Cities*, vol. 10, no. 3 (Aug. 1993), p. 237-42.
Before Slovenian independence, housing matters were decentralized, a large number of the people living in flats owned by the local *občine* (municipal councils). Since independence and changes in local government structures, a large amount of the housing stock, formerly privately owned, has been transferred back to private owners and house prices are now very high in Slovenia – often set in Deutschmarks – which has led to problems for younger families trying to establish themselves in the housing market.

417 **The unity of opposites in urban planning.**
Zdravko Mlinar. *International Journal of Urban and Regional Research*, vol. 2 (June 1978), p. 287-302.

Slovenian town planners have often been concerned to contrast the older heritage of their towns with newer innovative architecture. Very fine examples of these contrasts are to be found in Maribor and Ljubljana.

418 **A systems approach to town urban design: the case of Ljubljana.**
Andrej B. Pogačnik. *Town Planning Review*, vol. 48, no. 2 (1977), p. 187-92.

Pogačnik describes the 'masterplan' *Ljubljana 2000*, developed by a research team from the faculties of Civil Engineering, Architecture and Geodesy at Ljubljana University, using computer-aided visual models.

419 **Urban design: the case of Ljubljana.**
Andrej B. Pogačnik. *Town and Country Planning*, vol. 45 (Dec. 1977), p. 538-42.

Rapid urbanization ruined some of the aesthetic appeal of Yugoslavia's Gothic or Muslim towns. Ljubljana contains the architectural heritage of Sitte, Plečnik and Fabiani. Pogačnik discusses plans for improving Ljubljana's urban space, particularly in order to maximize 'the visual quality of the city' (p. 538).

420 **Slovenia: modernisation without urbanisation?**
D. I. Rusinow. *Common Ground*, vol. 1, no. 2 (1975), p. 57-70.

Dennison Rusinow, a leading American authority on the former Yugoslavia, considers how Slovenia could have achieved modernization of its economy without the growth of enormous urban conglomerations and the consequent environmental hazards.

421 **The sale of social housing stock in Slovenia: what happened and why.**
Tine Stanovnik. *Urban Studies*, vol. 31, no. 9 (Nov. 1994), p. 1559-70.

The Housing Act of 1991 provided a legal framework for all-encompassing housing reform. Social housing stock, which represented some 33 per cent of the total (about 100,000 dwellings) was transferred from tenant-occupied to owner-occupied status. Stanovnik considers that while privatization in this sphere has bought some short-term gains to sellers, it has also accentuated regional disparities. He takes examples from Novo mesto, Ljubljana, Maribor and Koper.

422 **Planning urban environment in a self-management society.**
Marija Vouk. The Hague: Institute of Social Studies, 1976. 58p.

From the early 1960s, the Republic of Slovenia had a self-management system that introduced elements of democratic decision-making into town planning. These elements are discussed here.

423   **The towns of Slovenia: some characteristics of their development
       and socioeconomic significance and of the urban network.**
       Igor Vriser.   *Geografski zbornik*, vol. 14 (1974), p. 135-52.

The towns of Slovenia are notable for their lack of industry, which is in the main
located outside the town centres, although there are exceptions such as Kranj. Most
are served by a bus network, although trains serve most of the major towns as well.

Rural planning

424   **Program issues in improving the quality of Slovene rural life.**
       Theodore Buila.   *Papers in Slovene Studies*, vol. 3 (1977), p. 83-104.

Buila looks at government attempts to improve the quality of rural life, including the
availability of education and other public services.

425   **Conservation planning within a framework of landscape planning
       in Slovenia.**
       J. Marušič.   *Landscape and Urban Planning*, vol. 23, nos. 3-4 (1993),
       p. 233-7.

Distinguishes three approaches to environmental protection or conservation activity,
which have been used simultaneously in Slovenia. Protection through land reserves
has achieved a central role, environmental impact assessments have been carried out
since the early 1970s, and in 1984 vulnerability analysis was also introduced in
Slovenia. Conflict is particularly apparent over the use of agricultural land space.

Environment protection

426   **Perception of the air pollution hazard in Ljubljana, Yugoslavia.**
       Daniel J. Basta.   In: *Environmental deterioration in the Soviet Union
       and Eastern Europe.*   Edited by Ivan Volges.   New York: Praeger,
       1974, p. 130-40.

In Ljubljana, the *slab zrak* (or *slab luft* in the local dialect) (bad air) is notorious and
generally blamed on pollution, although natural phenomena such as the marsh air from
the Ljubljansko barje may also be at fault.

427   **Analysis of residuals – environmental quality management: a case study of the Ljubljana area of Yugoslavia.**
Daniel J. Basta.   Washington, DC: Resources for the Future. 1978.
xxiv, 232p. maps. (RFF Research Paper, no. R-11).
Examines attempts to control air quality in Ljubljana through monitoring residuals.

428   **Environmental impact assessment legislation, Czech Republic, Estonia, Hungary, Latvia, Lithuania, Poland, Slovak Republic and Slovenia.**
London: Graham and Trotman, 1994. xv, 249p.
Published for the European Bank for Reconstruction and Development, it considers the legislation adopted to limit damage inflicted on the environment during the previous fifty years.

429   **From below: independent peace and environmental movements in Eastern Europe: a Helsinki Watch report.**
New York: Helsinki Watch Commitee, 1987. 263p.
Chapter six (p. 181-206) of this report is devoted to movements in Yugoslavia, and particularly Slovenia where the anti-nuclear power lobby and conscientious objectors have been active in recent years.

430   **Response to air pollution in Ljubljana, Yugoslavia.**
David E. Kromm.   *Annals of the Association of American Geographers*, vol. 63, no. 2 (June 1973), p. 208-17.
An exposition of the main sources of air pollution in the capital city of Slovenia, with an evaluation of the attempt at institutional monitoring and regulation of the hazards. The purpose of the paper is to suggest ways in which the reasonable level of public awareness can be translated into an effective community response.

431   **Zelena Knjiga o ogroženosti okolja v Sloveniji.** (The Green Book on the threat to the environment in Slovenia.)
Chief editor Stane Peterlin.   Ljubljana: Pridoslovno društvo, Slovenije, 1972. 255p. maps. bibliog.
A survey of the Slovenian environment under the subheadings of soil, water, air, plant life, animal life and man. The political importance of this survey was and remains immense as the Slovenians were arguably the most environmentally aware group in Communist Eastern Europe. (For instance, the Chernobyl disaster led to street demonstrations in Ljubljana.) Although the text is in Slovene, the main findings are summarized in English. Peterlin is also the editor of *Varstvo narave* (Nature conservation) (Ljubljana: Republican Institute for Nature Conservation) which has appeared annually in Slovene from 1962 to 1987 and again since 1987, with English summaries.

432   **Environmental public preferences as obtained by the method of photo-interpretation in the Ljubljana region.**
Andrej B. Pogačnik.   *Urban Education*, vol. 4, no. 1 (1979), p. 45-51.
An interesting example of how academic research intersects with public appearance, as Pogačnik explains new methods in urban planning as applied to Ljubljana.

433   **Study for the regulation and management of the Sava river in Yugoslavia: general report.**
New York: United Nations, 1972. 13 vols.
The Sava river has its source in the Alps near to the Italian border in Slovenia and flows through the outskirts of Ljubljana, down to Zagreb and Belgrade. At the time of this report, commissioned by the United Nations, it had important industrial uses. These have now been largely diminished by the war, but they are discussed in this study.

Education

School system

434 The development of education in the Republic of Slovenia 1990-92.
Jelka Arh. Ljubljana: Ministry of Education and Sport, Center for
Information and International Cooperation, 1992. 72p.

The work contains a brief description of the national education system divided into
pre-University education, higher (post-secondary) education, and sport education. The
author then considers significant changes and innovation in the post-Communist
period. Part 3 is the outline of a plan of action to eradicate illiteracy by the year 2000.

435 Slovenia's education in the process of change: legal aspects.
Leopoldina Plut-Pregelj. *Slovene Studies*, vol. 13, no. 2 (1991),
p. 129-41.

Deals with the changes to the educational system after April 1990 and the introduction
of a new constitution in December 1991. In the field of education, the restructuring
was accomplished by the law on the organization and financing of education, enacted
in September 1991.

**436 The effect of the Slovene preschool programme on the readiness of
children to begin school.**
Ivan Toličič. *International Journal of Early Childhood*, vol. 6, no. 2
(1974), p. 94-7.

The author compares the readiness to begin school of children who had attended
preschool programmes or 'little schools' in Litija and Tolmin, with those who had
attended just nursery.

437 **New approaches to educational planning in Slovenia.**
Monka Tratnik. Paris: International Institute for Educational
Planning (UNESCO), 1992. 30p. (Working Document).

Presents a short history of education in Slovenia and then summarizes how education
is planned with reference to the work of the Ministry of Education and Sport. Tratnik
makes observations on the importance of decentralization and information systems.

Higher education

438 **The Tempus Scheme – mobilizing higher education for change in
Central and Eastern Europe.**
Roger Absalom. *Educational and Training Technology International*,
vol. 30, no. 2 (1993), p. 122-8.

TEMPUS forms part of the EC aid for economic restructuring of the countries of
Central and Eastern Europe, known as PHARE. Because of the political and military
situation in the former Yugoslavia, only applications relating to Slovenia could be
considered. The article then describes the early phases of the scheme and the
participation of Slovenia. See also Jean Pierre Jallade, 'The role of education in the
renewal of the education and training systems of Central and Eastern Europe',
Educational and Training Technology International, vol. 30, no. 2 (1993), p. 113-21,
which describes the project to restructure the science curriculum in primary education
in Slovenia, which is being co-ordinated by the University of Ljubljana and funded by
TEMPUS.

439 **Information on policy direction in adult education in the Republic
of Slovenia.**
Olga Drofenik. Ljubljana: Andragoški center Republike Slovenije,
1994. 12p.

In 1994, only 0.4 per cent of the budget of the Ministry of Education and Sport was
spent on adult education. Nevertheless, new laws on Advanced Tertiary Education in
1993 created two planned national programmes (including a national plan for adult
education, with the the possibility of integration into the university sector). The Adult
Education Center (Andragoški center) was also founded and is in part government
funded. The pamphlet then provides information on the scope of adult education,
including location, student numbers, and current research.

440 **Education in multicultural societies.**
Ljubljana: Inštitut za Narodnostna Vprašanja. 441p.; *Razprave in
Gradivo*, vol. 18 (March 1986).

A collection of essays on multicultural schooling, mostly concerning Slovenia,
Slovene ethnic areas in Austria and Italy and the former Yugoslavia. Articles are in
French or English with English abstracts.

441   **The Slovenian matica, 1864: a modest enduring younger sister.**
Stanley B. Kimball.   In his: *The Austro-Slav revival.*   Philadelphia:
American Philosophical Society, 1973, p. 64-71.

The *matice* or literary societies founded amongst the Slavonic peoples of Eastern
Europe in the nineteenth century have played an enormous role in promoting native
culture and letters. Here Kimball assesses the importance of the Slovenska matica
founded in Ljubljana in 1864.

442   **Career plans and gender role attitudes of college students in the
United States, Japan and Slovenia.**
Yasuko Morinaga, Irene Hanson Frieze, Anuška Ferligoj.   *Sex Roles*,
vol. 29, no. 5-6 (1993), p. 317-34.

Compares students' career plans, work values and gender role attitudes in the United
States, Japan and Slovenia. The Slovenians were social science students, aged 20-22
(65 men and 92 women) and studying at Ljubljana University. On the whole,
Slovenian students were less worried about having time for their families than their
American and Japanese contemporaries, which suggests either a general economic
uncertainty or that career structures are more flexible.

443   **Education for the 21st century. Global conception of the
development of education in the Republic of Slovenia.**
Ferdo Rečnik.   Ljubljana: Zavod Republike Slovenije za šolstvo,
1991. 77p.

Outlines the education systems in Slovenia and contemporary strategies of permanent
education, dividing these into two parts: education of children or youth and education
of adults.

444   **Problems of introducing interdisciplinary and interfaculty studies
in the University of Ljubljana, Yugoslavia.**
Gojko Stanič.   *Higher Education*, vol. 4 (Feb. 1975), p. 61-5.

As Stanič explains, 'after a period of retreat into increasing specialisation in science
and research work, there has been a gradual movement back into the university as a
whole' (p. 63). He then explains the problems of this transition given the size of
Slovenia, the dominance of Ljubljana University, and the political climate at that time.

Science and Technology

445 **Magnetic resonance and relaxation, new fields and techniques.**
Edited by R. Blinc, M. Vilfan, J. Slak.   Ljubljana: J. Štefan Inštitut,
334p.

These are the proceedings of the 10th Ampere Summer School and Symposium held
in Portorož, 4-10 September 1988.

446 **Nonlinear seismic analysis and design of reinforced concrete
buildings.**
Edited by P. Fajfar, H. Krawinkler.   London: Elsevier Science
Publishers, 1992. vii, 307p.

Proceedings of the Workshop on Nonlinear Seismic Analysis of reinforced concrete
buildings, held in Bled in 1992.

447 **Spominski Zbornik Antona Kuhlja / Anton Kuhelj memorial
volume.**
Edited by Peter Gosar, Lujo Skuljc.   Ljubljana: Slovenska akademija
umetnosti in znanosti, 1982. 348p.

Anton Kuhelj's most distinguished field of research was the elastomechanics of plates
and shells. The results of this research were successfully applied to the construction of
gliders and various types of light planes. After the war, he worked at the Aeronautical
Institute in Zemun and then became Professor Emeritus of the University of Ljubljana,
two years before his death in 1980. This volume, a *Festschrift*, brings together the
work of his students in various fields of engineering. All the texts are in English with
Slovene summaries.

448   **Science in Slovenia.**
      Edited by Tamara Lah, Radko Osredar.   Ljubljana: Ministry of
      Science and Technology, 1992. 3rd ed., revised by Barbara Zupan.
      74p.

A brief history of science in Slovenia, which concentrates on the contemporary period,
but including the Enlightenment mathematician Jurij Vega, here credited with being
the inventor of logarithms.

449   **Optimal electric power conservation investments using utility**
      avoided costs.
      J. Renar, M. Tomšič.   *Energy*, vol. 17, no. 5 (1992), p. 499-508.

The authors describe the recent projects to conserve energy in Slovenia, including
hydroelectric power.

Literature

History and criticism

450   **A history of Yugoslav literature.**
Antun Barac, translated by Petar Mijusković.   Ann Arbor: Michigan
Slavic Publications, 1973. 266p.

An old but valuable history that includes assessments of Slovene writers.

451   **The national and the universal in Slovene literature.**
France Bernik. *Slovene Studies*, vol. 14, no. 2 (1992), p. 125-31.

Discusses the role of language in Slovene national literature. Both Prešeren and
Cankar had a German-language education and spent a great deal of time in German-
speaking milieux, but were nevertheless founders of their own national literatures,
whereas Stanko Vraz became known as a Croatian author and Louis Adamič as an
American. Bernik then goes on to discuss the role of symbolism. In an earlier article,
'The introduction of symbolism to Slovene literature', *Slovene Studies*, vol. 10, no. 2
(1988), p. 161-9, Bernik considers the role of symbolism in the work of Ivan Cankar,
Oton Župančič and other writers of the Slovene Moderna movement.

452   **France Prešeren.**
Henry Ronald Cooper.   Boston, Massachusetts: Twayne, 1981. 169p.
bibliog.

As Cooper says, France Prešeren (1800-49) was both 'the champion and victim of his
language'. Born in Radovljica he became the leading figure of a group of literati in
Ljubljana, which included his friend Matija Čop, to whom he dedicated poetry.
Although Prešeren also wrote in German, it was his poetry in Slovene that was to
become the standard for all subsequent work in the Slovene language. The poem
Zdravljica (A toast), which became the Slovenian national anthem, rises above the
parochialism of nationalism or even Pan-Slavism to represent a universal anthem, a
toast to mankind. Nevertheless, Prešeren's work can still be placed within the time in
which it was written. In *Krst pri Savici* (Baptism on the Savica), Prešeren invented an

epic hero Črtomir in direct imitation of South Slav oral poetry. Cooper's book combines the functions of a biography and a criticism of Prešeren's work. The work is grouped according to genre: lyric poems, ballads and romances, sonnets, the German poems. Of related interest is Igor I. Schillich, 'France Prešeren, the unknown genius, 1800-1849. The poet, the nation and his place in world literature' (PhD dissertation, Vanderbilt University, 1972. 601p.).

453 Župančič and Whitman.
Henry R. Cooper. *Southeastern Europe*, vol. 9, nos. 1-2 (1982), p. 147-59.

A special edition of this periodical on Yugoslavian literature edited by Vasa D. Mihailovich. In this article, Henry Cooper considers one of the enduring myths of Slovenian literary criticism, namely whether Oton Župančič was influenced by Walt Whitman? He concludes, in partial agreement with Janko Kos, that autonomous influences on Župančič's creativity were more important. For a more detailed study of Župančič, see Lucien Tesnière, *Oton Joupantchitch. Poète slovène* (Paris: Belles-lettres, 1931. 383p.).

454 Oton Župančič and Slovene modernism.
Henry Ronald Cooper. *Slovene Studies*, vol. 13, no. 1 (1991), p. 3-18.

Cooper argues that Župančič's work personifies the Slovene Moderna movement.

455 The waste land in a state of siege: comments on the contemporary Slovene novel.
Milena Davidson. *Slovene Studies*, vol. 3, no. 2 (1981), p. 72-86.

Focuses on four contemporary novelists: Rudi Šeligo, Andrej Hieng, Miha Remec and Dimitrij Rupel. She argues that 'Rupel, like Hieng and Remec and to a lesser degree Šeligo, sees history as a cycle, where revolutions are nothing more than the full turns of a circle . . . The picaresque quest for some unspecified utopia is then doomed from the start' (p. 83). Thus does literature become contemporary politics.

456 Yugoslav camp literature: rediscovering the ghost of a nation's past–present–future.
Oskar Gruenwald. *Slavic Review*, vol. 46, nos. 3-4 (1984), p. 513-28.

When Yugoslavia was expelled from Cominform in 1948, pro-Stalinists were rounded up for re-education, largely on the Adriatic island of Goli otok, which subsequently became a symbol for the repression of the Titoist regime. The Slovene writer Vitomil Zupan was amongst those imprisoned and the importance of their literary production is discussed here. For a Slovene perspective on the prison camps for Cominternists, see Božidar Jezernik, 'Non cogito ergo sum: arheologija neke šale' (I do not think therefore I am: the archaeology of a joke), *Revija za Zgodovino, Literaturo in Antropologijo*, vol. 46 (1994), p. 655-856.

457 **Poems of the Slovene Moderna.**
Peter Herrity. In: *Russian and Yugoslav culture in the age of modernism.* Edited by Cynthia Marsh, Wendy Rosslyn. Nottingham: Astra Press, 1991, p. 123-32.
Translations and commentaries of the poems of Cankar and Župančič.

458 **Australian papers: Yugoslavia, Europe and Australia.**
Edited by Mirko Jurak. Ljubljana: Edvard Kardelj University of Ljubljana, Faculty of Arts and Science, 1983. 321p.
A publication arising from a conference on Australian Studies held at Bled, Slovenia, in 1982 and dealing with Yugoslav–Australian cultural relations and studies of the Slovene diaspora.

459 **Some specific themes of contemporary Slovenian poetry.**
Ante Kadić. *Journal of Croatian Studies*, nos. 14-15 (1973-74), p. 145-56.
Analyses themes in the poetry of Oton Župančič (1878-1949), Alojž Gradnik (1882-1967), Edvard Kocbek (1904-80) and Dane Zajc (1929-), who are all said to have introduced themes concerning universal human problems into their poetry.

460 **'Death of a villager': by J. Kerstnik. A reflection on death in literature.**
Ante Kadić. *Slovene Studies*, vol. 4, no. 1 (1982), p. 15-20.
Janko Kerstnik (1852-97) was a writer of the realist period, who became known for his depictions of rural life such as *Kmetske slike* (Peasant sketches, 1882-91). In *Kmetska smrt* (Death of a peasant, 1890), where the hero Planjavec dies after falling into a fire after an epileptic fit and is administered the last rites, Kerstnik is said to give an extraordinary insight into the peasant's attitude towards his own death. As Kadić says, 'we should behave like Kerstnik's Planjavec: when the old man hears that he will die, the words did not appear so terrible; on the contrary – they sounded to him as a relief (*kakor tolažilo*)' (p. 20).

461 **Homer and Slovene culture.**
Gander Kajetun. *Balkan Studies*, vol. 10, no. 10 (1969), p. 225-50.
'The beginnings of Homer's influence on Slovene artistic creativity are veiled in the mists of illiteracy, spun in a net of invisible, scarcely discernable threads, which are not likely ever to be disentangled or definitely identified' (p. 25). The similarities between Homeric and Slovene folk-songs struck the author, but he contents himself with assessing the effects on literature. He argues that the 'torrent' found in France Prešeren's *Krst pri Savici* (Baptism on the Savica) is found in the *Iliad* in at least seven places. The nineteenth century mocked his friend Andrej Kragelj, who translated Homer thus: 'Quick, Andrej, mount Pegasus, thou Odysseus, for this will be better than all the sharp wits of Prešeren, and the whole of Slovenia will astound' (p. 240).

462   **France Prešeren, 1800-49.**
Janko Lavrin.   *Slavonic and East European Review*, vol. 33, no. 81 (1955), p. 304-27.

A brief critical outline of the life and poetry of Slovenia's first major poet. For a more extensive treatment of this subject, see Anton Slodnjak, *France Prešeren* (Ljubljana: Slovenska matica, 1962. 328p.).

463   **On the options of the poetry of a small nation.**
Rado L. Lenček.   *Slovene Studies*, vol. 1, no. 1 (1979), p. 4-13.

Lenček questions the role of Slovene work within world literature. 'Slovenes', he argues, 'are one of the tiniest natural units in Europe: yet they have withstood all the calamities of history and today possess a literature quite out of proportion to their size' (p. 5-6). He sees the greatness of Slovene poetry in part in its triumph over 'provincialism', enabling the poetry of Prešeren, for example, to transcend beyond local borders.

464   **The beginnings of modern Slovene literary scholarship.**
Kresimir Nemec.   *Slovene Studies*, vol. 5, no. 2 (1983), p. 189-206.

Assesses the importance of the Slovene Moderna (modernism), also known as Neo-Romanticism (1899-1918), particularly the work of Ivan Prijatelj (1875-1937). Although litarary scholarship can arguably be dated from the work of Primož Trubar in the sixteenth century, it was at the beginning of the twentieth century that it 'reached a key transitional point' (p. 193).

465   **Emigrants in Ivan Cankar's fiction.**
Irma M. Ožbalt.   *Slovene Studies*, vol. 4, no. 2 (1982), p. 99-112.

Cankar's emigrant stories date from the first years of this century. He was preoccupied not only with the 'proletarianisation' of the Slovene lands, but with emigration to America. He also created naturalistic portrayals of Czech immigrants in Vienna. In general, Cankar did not dwell on those who were successful but on the misery of exile, especially for children. He seems to have believed that it was easier to suffer amongst one's own than amongst strangers.

466   **The theme of the unwed mother in Slovene literature.**
Marija A. I. Ožbalt.   *Slovene Studies*, vol. 3, no. 2 (1981), p. 59-71.

Consistently one of the most creative and original writers about Slovene culture, here Ožbalt compares three writers who dwelt on the theme of the unmarried mother in their prose: France Prešeren's *Nezakonska mati*, written in the 1840s, Ivan Cankar's *Polikarp*, *Smrt in pogreb Jakoba nesreče* and *Aleš iz Razora*, and Prežihov Voranc's *Samorastniki*. As Ožbalt writes, 'persecution of unmarried mothers and their helpless children was one of the outstanding injustices that all three writers witnessed in the society of their time. Prešeren was touched by it through personal tragedy; Cankar's keen eye for social evil born of ignorance, notices it in the small town of Vrhnika as well as in the slums of Vienna, Voranc saw it among the sturdy peasants of the Carinthian mountains whose passion for life mingled with mediaeval attitudes and fear and made them victims of their own ignorance' (p. 68).

467   **The myth of America in Slovene literature up to the Second World War.**
Jerneja Petrič.   *Slovene Studies*, vol. 13, no. 1 (1991), p. 101-6.
Discusses the symbolic meaning of 'America' in Slovene literature, including the work of Ivan Cankar and Janez Cigler. Of related interest, see also Andrej Vovko, 'The myth of America and the society of St. Raphael', *Slovene Studies*, vol. 13, no. 1 (1991), p. 107-10; and Mirko Jurak, 'The new world In Etbin Kristin's plays', *Melus*, vol. 12 (Winter 1985), p. 53-61.

468   **Childhood in the works of Ivan Tavčar: a comparison of the early works and the novel *Visoška Kronika*.**
Timothy Pogacar.   *Slovene Studies*, vol. 10, no. 2 (1988), p. 149-60.
Tavčar's work concerns family life in the region of Škofja loka in the nineteenth century. Ivan Tavčar's work is not yet translated in any quantity in English, so the main source for his work remains his *Zbrano delo* (Collected works) (Ljubljana: Državna založba Slovenije, 1951-58. 7 vols).

469   **The heresy of Edvard Kocbek.**
Dimitrij Rupel.   *Slovene Studies*, vol. 10, no. 1 (1988), p. 51-60.
The poet Edvard Kocbek is normally described as a Christian Socialist, but he was critical both of the Catholic Church and of the League of Communists. Rupel therefore describes his politics as 'heretical' and illustrates this with examples of what he calls his 'paradigmatic political acts', such as his 1951 book *Strah in pogum* (Fear and courage), which broke with socialist realist tradition and was heavily criticized at the time. Rupel also mentions his interview with the Triestine newspaper *Žaliv* in 1975, in which he discussed the slaughter of the Domobranci in 1975. Of related interest is Helga Glušič, 'The poetry and prose of Edvard Kocbek (1904-81)', *Slovene Studies*, vol. 8, no. 2 (1986), p. 65-71. Dimitrij Rupel also wrote his doctoral thesis on the importance of literature, see 'Slovene literature as an instrument of national emanicipation' (Brandeis University, Ann Arbor, Michigan, 1976. 547p.).

470   **Regionalism versus Europeanism as leading concepts in the works of Srečko Kosovel.**
Peter Scherber.   *Slovene Studies*, vol. 13, no. 2 (1991), p. 155-66.
In 1923 the Karst poet Srečko Kosovel wrote to a friend, *'moje življenje je moje, slovensko, sodobno, evropsko in večno'* ('my life is mine, Slovene, contemporary, European and more'). Scherber examines the role of the Karst (*kras*), which he describes as a bucolic landscape and in terms of an idyll. The intermediate space, Ljubljana, stands for Kosovel's confrontation with Slovene patriotism (*slovenstvo*). For him *slovenstvo* should be the political task of the ordinary workers and peasants, not the petit-bourgeoisie in Ljubljana. The third level for Kosovel was 'the outside world', that is Yugoslavia and Europe. He was critical of Yugoslavia, especially Croat lack of accommodation, and treats the League of Nations in Geneva as 'the European lie', anticipating instead 'the construction of a new, humane life' (p. 164). On regionalism in Slovene literature, see also Miran Hladnik, 'Regionalism in Slovene rural prose', *Slovene Studies*, vol. 13, no. 2 (1991), p. 143-53.

471   **Fran Levstik (1831-1887) the first representative of realism in
       Slovene literature.**
       Anton Slodnjak.   *Slavonic and East European Review*, vol. 35, no. 84
       (1956), p. 24-40.

Levstik was one of the most important men of letters in the nineteenth century in the
Slovene lands. As secretary of Slovenska matica he brought the influence of Heine and
Goethe to his compatriots. One of his greatest achievements was the novella *Martin
Krpan* in which folkloric motives were moulded into a realistic literature. Fran
Levstik's entire work was published as *Zbrano delo* (Ljubljana: Državna založba
Slovenije, 1948-61. 9 vols).

472   **A survey of modern Slovene literature.**
       Josip Vidmar.   *Slavonic and East European Review*, vol. 6, no. 18
       (March 1928), p. 618-34.

A survey of the canon of Slovene literature, by an ardent promoter of his national
culture. As Vidmar writes, 'If we can apply to Prešern [sic], Kant's definition of the
"sublime" (*erhaben*), another expression of the same philosopher is better suited to
Župančič: his work is splendid (*prachtig*) – splendid, however, in the best sense of the
word . . . Župančič is the greatest authority in the Slovene language, and its most
perfect master of form. He and Cankar have perfected it and brought it to the extreme
limit of expression' (p. 630).

473   **The krakowiak in Croatian and Slovene poetry.**
       Ivana Živanković-Sekarus.   *Slavonic and East European Review*,
       vol. 71, no. 2 (April 1993), p. 278-86.

The krakowiak is a Polish national dance combined with a song, performed with a
syncopated rhythm. Both Slovene and Croatian verse during the nineteenth century –
especially that with romantic themes – are influenced by the Polish original.
Živanković-Sekarus argues that the the poet Stanko Vraz (1812-51) introduced the
form to Slovene and Croatian literature, both in his cycle of poems 'Djulabije' (Rose
apples) published in Zagreb in 1840, and in his earlier Slovene poems dating from the
mid-1930s. The krakowiak form was inherited by others in Croat and Slovene
literature, including Simon Jenko (1835-69).

Trends and major writers

474   **A wanderer in the atom age.**
       Matej Bor, translated from the Slovene by Janko Lavrin, with an
       introduction by B. Borko, illustrated by Nora Lavrin.   Ljubljana:
       Državna založba Slovenije. 69p.

A poet of the Slovene modernist movement, Matej Bor (the pseudonym of Vladimir
Pavšič) abandonned the expressionist style that characterized Slovene poetry before
1914. Influenced by Oton Župančič, he produced an 'individually coloured realistic

lyricism, without any linguistic obscurities' (B. Borko, p. 5). This bilingual edition, sumptuously illustrated with black-and-white drawings by Nora Lavrin dwells on the metaphorical journey of 'a wanderer in the atom age [who] reached the border of Being and non-Being' (p. 69).

475 The bailiff Yerney and his rights.

Ivan Cankar, translated from the Slovene by Sidonie Yeras, H. C. Sewell Grant, introduced by Janko Lavrin.   London: Rodker, 1930. 114p. Reprinted, with illustrations by Nora Lavrin, London: Pushkin, 1946.

This allegorical novel, heavily critical of the Habsburg *ancien régime*, is considered to one of the finest pieces of prose by Ivan Cankar (1876-1918). Like Heinrich von Kleist's fictional character Michael Kohlhaas, the baillif Yerney is determined to have justice at any price when his master sacks him. When his attempts to see his rights honoured fail, he burns down his old master's house in a desperate attempt to right the wrong done to him.

476 Slovene idylls.

Ivan Cankar.   *Slavonic and East European Review*, vol. 13, no. 39 (April 1935), p. 494-506.

A selection of short, episodic stories by the master of the Slovene Moderna. Cankar's stories 'I know how, Mother' and 'Simple Martin' were also published in *Slavonic and East European Review*, vol. 17, no. 49 (July 1938), p. 35-41.

477 The ward of Our Lady of Mercy.

Ivan Cankar, translated by Henry Leeming.   Ljubljana: Državna založba Slovenije, 1976. 133p.

A short novel, which contrasts the bright spirit of a dying child Malchie with the gloomy hospital where she has gone to die. The other thirteen children in the sick ward are used to create particular dramatic portraits of social groups who suffered in the twilight years of the Habsburg monarchy, such as the proletarian Tina and the Jewish Pauline. Based on the suffering of Amalia Loeffler, a child known to Cankar who had tuberculosis, this novel dwells metaphorically on the unhappy health of *fin-de-siècle* Vienna.

478 My life.

Ivan Cankar, selected and introduced by Josip Vidmar, translated by Elza Jereb, Alasdair MacKinnon.   Murska sobota, Slovenia: Pomorski tisk, for Mladinska knjiga International, 1988. 127p.

Beautifully translated selection of the short stories of Slovenia's finest prose writers, including the poignant 'Cup of coffee' where the author recalls a moment when he snubbed his mother and which he regretted greatly afterwards. For an earlier English-language compilation of Cankar short stories, see *Dream visions, and other selected stories*, translated from the Slovene by Anton Družina, illustrated with prints and drawings by Lillian Brulc (Willoughby Hills, Ohio: Slovenian Research Centre of America, 1982. 202p.). See also Milena Davidson, 'Ivan Cankar: translation of four novellas with introductions' (PhD dissertation, University of Maryland, 1982. 152p.).

479 **Anxious moments.**
Aleš Debeljak, translated from the Slovene by Christopher Merill with the author, and with a preface by Charles Simic. Fredonia, New York: White Pine Press, 1994. 78p.

Poetry by one of Slovenia's finest contemporary writers. Debeljak is also an active writer on literary matters; see, for example, 'Writers and politicians: a necessary divorce in the wake of independence', *Slovene Studies*, vol. 13, no. 2 (1991), p. 191-4. See also his 'Literature against the politics of oblivion', *Slovene Studies*, vol. 10, no. 1 (1988), p. 61-4, in which he considers, amongst other things the literary themes in Vitomil Zupan's *Levitan* (Ljubljana: Cankarjeva založba, 1982).

480 **Thirty years of Yugoslav literature (1945-1975).**
Thomas Eekman. Ann Arbor: Michigan Slavic Publications, 1978. 328p.

The three chronological sections of Eekman's account are also divided by republic, providing an accessible survey of Slovene literature of this period by an acknowledged American authority. The anthology *New writing in Yugoslavia*. Edited by Bernard Johnson (Harmondsworth, England: Penguin, 1970. 342p.) also includes Slovene writers.

481 **Buried in the sands of time.**
Janko Ferk, translated by Herbert Kuhner. Riverside, California: Ariadne Press, 1989. 62p.

Janko Ferk (1958-), a Carinthian writer whose prose and poetry is notable for its engagement with contemporary philosophy and its use of irony, appears here in a trilingual English/Slovene/German edition of his poetry. See also *Koroška slovenska poezija / Carinthian Slovenian poetry*. Edited by Felix J. Bišter and Herbert Kuhner (Klagenfurt, Austria: [n.p.], 1984. 216p.), which introduces the work of fourteen contemporary poets to the outside world.

482 **Repetition.**
Peter Handke, translated by Ralph Mannheim. London: Methuen; New York: Farrar, Straus and Giroux, 1988. 246p.

Handke, one of Austria's leading playwrights, is himself half-Slovene. In this semi-autobiography (A translation of *Die Wiederholung* [Frankfurt am Main: Verlag Suhrkamp, 1992. 334p.]), he describes the Slovene language with great beauty. For a discussion of Handke's work, see Michael Biggins, 'Handke's Slovenia and Šalamun's America: the literary uses of Utopia', *Slovene Studies*, vol. 13, no. 2 (1991), p. 181-90.

483 **Death at Mary-of-the-Snows.**
Drago Jančar. *Slavic and East European Arts*, vol. 2, no. 2 (Spring 1984), p. 99-108.

The story of a Russian doctor Vladimir Semyanov in inter-war Slovenia by a leading Slovenian writer. This special edition of the journal, subtitled 'The mythmakers: an anthology of contemporary Yugoslav short stories', selected and translated by Mario Suško and Edward J. Czerwinski, also includes 'The earth' by Branko Gradišnik (p. 123-8).

484 **The day Tito died.**
Drago Jančar, Brane Gradišnik, Jani Virk, Lela B. Njatin, Andrej
Blatnik. London: Forest Books, 1993. 149p.

The first anthology of Slovenian short stories (other than the work of Cankar) to be published in English, this represents some of the finest work of the younger generation of Slovene writers who have emerged as an intellectual force since the mid-1980s, as well as the work of the more established writer Drago Jančar, whose work is well known outside Slovenia. In the title story Andrej Blatnik explains from a personal perspective how it was that the legends of the partisans passed into memory. Perhaps this is the overwhelming significance of this collection.

485 **Na vratih zvecer / At the door at evening.**
Edvard Kocbek, translated by Tom Ložar. Dorian, Quebec: The
Muses Company/La Compagnie des Muses; Ljubljana: Aleph, 1990.
116p.

Born in 1904, Kocbek was one of the major Slovene poets of the twentieth century. Initially he studied for the priesthood and fought alongside the partisans in the Liberation Front after 1941. A committed Christian Socialist, he was a critic of the Communist regime, although he had been a government functionary during the post-war reconstruction period. In this selection of 47 of his poems, the reader is introduced to Kocbek's world – divided into 'before' (the Second World War), 'during' and 'after'. In *V seminarju* (In the seminar), he speculates what would happen if seven million Chinese all jumped a height of two metres. He continues, 'We, Slovenians, for instance, would need to jump from such a height that we would all be killed. That is why we have to sign up with our neighbours' (p. 111).

486 **Silence of stone (kamen molka). Selected poetry.**
Andrej Kokot, translated by Franc Šehović, introduced by Ivan Dolenc.
Toronto, Ontario: Yugoslav Canadian Publishers, 1987. 109p.

Andrej Kokot (1936-) is a Carinthian Slovene whose melancholy and terse, bitter style is reflected in his work. This collection features 35 of his lyrics in a bilingual Slovene and English edition.

487 **A day in spring.**
Ciril Kosmač, translated by Fanny S. Copeland. London: Lincolns-
Prager, 1959. 205p.

Ciril Kosmač (1910-80) came from the Karst area to Slovenia and also had a parallel career as a journalist and film director. Readers will be struck by his forthright and almost autobiographical style as this novel deals with the impact of pain and suffering on the writer. The theme of the novel, which was made into a film and is rightly regarded as one of the best novels emanating from the post-war milieu in Slovenia, concerns the pregnancy of a woman who has had a liaison with an Italian soldier when she herself was the product of a similar liaison during the First World War The Slovene ethnic lands have been partitioned and divided among eight different state formations during the twentieth century. In part this is a novel about the impact of this political chaos on ordinary lives.

488 **Integrals.**
Srečko Kosovel, translated, introduced and selected by Wilhelm
Heliger. Santa Barbara, California: Mudborn Place, 1983. 120p.
A selection of poetry by the leading poet of the Karst region.

489 **An anthology of modern Yugoslav poetry in English translations.**
Edited with a preface by Janko Lavrin. London: Calder, 1962. 200p.
A representative selection from Yugoslav poets of the twentieth century, selected by a
distinguished Slovene critic.

490 **Death of a simple giant, and other modern Yugoslav stories.**
Edited by Branko Lenski. New York: Vanguard, 1965. 306p.
Includes the work of the Slovene writers Prežihov Voranc and Ciril Kosmač. Another
collection – *Yugoslav short stories.* Selected, translated and introduced by Svetozar
Koljević (London: Oxford University Press, 1966. 380p. [World's Classics, no. 608])
– includes the work of Ivan Cankar.

491 **Slovene poets of today.**
Edited by Janez Menart, with a preface by Filip Kalan, translated by
Alasdair Mackinnon. Ljubljana: Druzba slovenskih pisatelj, 1965.
151p.
An anthology of post-war Slovene poets, including Edvard Kocbek and Janez Menart.

492 **Contemporary Yugoslav poetry.**
Edited by Vasa D. Mihailovich, introduced by Gertrud Graubert-Champe.
Iowa City: University of Iowa Press, 1977. 242p.
An anthology, which includes the work of Edvard Kocbek, Ciril Zlobec, Dane Zajc,
Tomaž Šalamun, Gregor Strniša, Tone Pavcek, Veno Taufer, Kajetan Kovič and Cene
Vipotnik.

493 **Five modern Yugoslav plays.**
Edited and introduced by Branko Mikaksinovich. New York: Cyrco,
1977. 339p.
Includes a translation of 'An affair' (*Afera*) by Primož Kozak (p. 86-145) which
'describes the vigours of combat, guerrilla authority and discipline and the conflict
between a group of idealistic and anarchic freedom fighters and their sympathetic, but
level-headed commander' (p. 86).

494 **Modern Yugoslav satire.**
Edited and introduced by Branko Mikaksinovich. Merrick, New
York: Cross-Cultural Communications, 1979. 204p.
The collection includes satire by the Slovenian writers Tomaž Šalamun and Žarko
Petan.

495 **Introduction to Yugoslav literature: an anthology of fiction and poetry.**
Edited by Branko Mikaksinovich, Dragan Milivojević, Vasa D. Mihailovich. New York: Twayne, 1973. 647p.
A comprehensive anthology of the literature of the peoples of former Yugoslavia, which includes thirteen Slovene writers.

496 **The land and the flesh.**
Ivan Potrč, translated from the Slovene by Henry Leeming. London: Peter Owen, 1969. 263p.
Outstanding example of realism in Slovenian literature, this gloomy novels dwells on the problems of family relations, lust and murder on a small farm in the Eastern region of Prekmurje.

497 **Vicar Mathias' last guest.**
Ivan Pregelj. *Slavonic and East European Review*, vol. 13, no. 37 (July 1934), p. 27-35.
The story of the death of an old priest by a minor Slovene modernist writer.

498 **Selection of poems.**
France Prešeren, translated from the Slovene, edited by William K. Matthews, Anton Slodnjak. Oxford: Blackwell, 1954. 75p. 2nd ed., London: John Calder, 1963. 83p.
Originally published between 1830 and 1847, this volume presents a selection of the some of poetry by Slovenia's leading poet. The volume is introduced by Anton Slodnjak, a leading authority on the history of Slovene literature, who assesses Prešeren's life and his influence on historical developments. See also a translation of the Slovene national anthem *Zdravljica*, undertaken by K. Matthews, 'A toast, two sonnets and the unmarried mother', *Slavonic and East European Review*, vol. 27, no. 69 (1949), p. 335-44.

499 **The selected poems of Tomaž Šalamun.**
Edited by Charles Simič with an introduction by Robert Hass. New York: Ecco Press, 1988. xxviii, 93p.
Tomaž Šalamun, one of the most distinguished Slovene poets of the post-war generation, is said to have a penchant for self-mythologization in his work, finding the extraordinary in ordinary everyday encounters. His work has expanded the horizons of Slovene poetry, drawing on diverse sources from different artistic genres. See also his *The shepherd, the hunter*, translated with an introduction by Sonja Kravanja (Santa Fe, New Mexico: [n.p.], 1992. 86p.).

500 **Modern poetry in translation: Slovenia.**
Edited and translated by Veno Taufer, Michael Scammell. *Modern Poetry in Translation* (London), no. 8 (Sept. 1970). 30p.
Sponsored by the Arts Council of Great Britain, this special edition of the journal presents the work of fifteen poets from post-war Slovenia.

501 **The self-sown: bilingual edition of a Slovene classic.**
Prežihov Voranc, translated and introduced by Irma M. Ožbalt. New
Orleans, Louisiana: Založba Prometej, 1983. 111p.

Lovro Kuhar (1893-1950), who wrote under the pseudonym of Voranc, stemmed from
a peasant family in Ravna in Carinthia. Before the Second World War he was an
active journalist and socialist and as a result spent the war years in prison. After the
war he found favour with the Titoist regime for his political sympathies and his work
became part of a politically correct canon. This extraordinary book, spendidly
translated by Irma Ožbalt, is a story about the Carinthian peasantry from which he
sprang. It concerns the trials of an unwed mother who is cast out of the family with
whom she worked as a servant when she becomes pregnant by the oldest son. It is
apparently set in the nineteenth century, but in a sense this exact chronology is not
important. What is significant here is that the story is about the 'bad old feudal days'
when personal relations were subverted by concerns for inheritance. The characters
are barely developed and the almost naive style shows little influence of Freud's ideas.
Samorastniki (a term which is difficult to render into English but 'self-sown' conveys
the idea) was first published in Ljubljana in 1940. In this edition the Slovene text and
the English version are presented in parallel.

502 **Minuet for (25-shot) guitar.**
Vitomil Zupan, translated by Harry Leeming. Murska sobota,
Slovenia: Pomorski tisk, for Mladinska knjiga International, 1988.
317p.

This novel has two main locations: amongst the partisans fighting to regain Krim and
Mokrc nearby to Ljubljana from 1943 to 1945; and in postwar Spain. The protagonist
Jakob Bergant-Berk recalls his meeting with a former German enemy Joseph Bitter,
which leads him to speculate on the purpose of war. A strikingly metaphysical piece,
approaching an established literary theme in an unconventional manner.

503 **A selection of poems.**
Oton Župančič, edited by Janko Lavrin. Ljubljana: Državna založba
Slovenije, 1967. 51p.

A sample of the work of Oton Župančič, the literary giant of his generation and
translator of Shakespeare, second only to Prešeren as Slovenia's major poet.

The Arts

General

504 **Les arts en Slovénie.** (The arts in Slovenia.)
L'Oeil (Paris), no. 473 (July-Aug. 1995). 92p.

A special issue of this international arts magazine devoted to Slovenian art past and present, which also serves as a general historical introduction with lavish colour illustrations. As a whole the magazine emphasizes how important artistic creativity has been to the Slovenes. The collection includes an article, 'La photographie slovène' by Brane Kovič (p. 62-80) and an interview with Zoran Mušič (p. 82-3), an artist and writer who was born in Gorizia, by the French critic Patrick-Gilles Persin.

Architecture

505 **Jože Plečnik. Architect 1872-1957.**
Edited by Francois Burkhardt, Claude Eveno, Boris Podrecca, translated by Carol Volk. Cambridge, Massachusetts: MIT Press, 1989. 191p.

Introduces the work of Jože Plečnik, which is to be found across Europe, but particularly in Ljubljana, Prague, and Vienna. See also *Žale by Architect Jože Plečnik*. Text by Damjan Prelovšek (Ljubljana: Ljubljansko mesto, 1992. 159p.), which examines the architecture of the well-known cemetery.

506 **Plečnik: the complete works.**
Peter Krečič. London: Academy Press, 1993. 256p.

A comprehensive survey of Plečnik's work, including architecture, internal and external design, and monumental work. It locates Plečnik not only as a representative of the Slovenian Moderna movement, but also as an internationally significant Modernist. There are 328 illustrations.

507 **Church of the Sacred Heart: Jože Plečnik.**
I. Margolius, with photographs by M. Fiennes. London: Phaidon, 1995. 60p.

A detailed study of Plečnik's Church of the Sacred Heart, built in the Vinohrady quarter of Prague and described by the author as 'a characteristic Plečnik work, synthesising classical, Modernist and traditional Slovenian elements to create a building of great architectural force' (p. i). Every detail of Plečnik's design is photographed, and internal and external plans are also included.

508 **Contemporary architecture in Slovenia.**
A. Monfried. *Architecture – the AIA Journal*, vol. 81, no. 1 (1992), p. 19.

Ljubljana is a city where traditional styles, mostly from the Baroque period mix successfully with the more recent work of Maks Fabiani and Jože Plečnik. This article looks at the development of recent Slovenian architecture, particularly in Ljubljana, in the context of this rich historical legacy.

509 **The cathedral of Ljubljana.**
Maja Smole, translated by Janko Golias. Ljubljana: Parish Office of the Cathedral, 1982. 24p.

The Baroque spire of Ljubljana's St Nicholas Cathedral dates from the early eighteenth century although parts of the building were built as early as the fifteenth. It is one of the pearls of this beautiful town and has recently been restored to its full glory.

510 **Jože Plečnik in Ljubljana.**
Richard D. Wilson. *Progressive Architecture*, vol. 66, no. 10 (Oct. 1985), p. 96-103.

Looks at the innovative work of Slovenia's finest architect within Ljubljana. Of related interest is the illustrated *Jože Plečnik: architecture and the city*. Edited by Ian Bentley and Djurdja Gržarc-Butina (Oxford: Department of Urban Design, Oxford Polytechnic, 1983. 64p.).

511 **Romanesque architecture in Slovenia.**
Marjan Zadnikar. *Journal of the Society of Architectural Historians*, vol. 28, no. 2 (May 1969), p. 99-114.

Looks at medieval church architecture in Slovenia, which is largely to be found in the littoral region.

Visual arts

512 **Janez Boljka: sculpture and graphics.**
Janez Boljka, with a foreword by Zoran Kržišnik, translated from
Slovene by Dejan Sušnik, Martin Gregreen. Ljubljana: Cankarjeva
založba, 1986. 128p.
Janez Boljka (1931-) is one of Slovenia's finest sculptors whose statue of an
elongated and emaciated Ivan Cankar (1972) is well known. His work in bronze is
particularly distinguished. Animals, especially fish, are important themes in his work
and his human figures are often portrayed as primitive and bestial.

513 **Treasures of Slovenia.**
Matjaž Kmecl, translated by Margaret Davis, Stanko Klinar.
Ljubljana: Cankarjeva založba, 1981. 335p.
'Coffee table'-format book of architectural and artistic heritage in Slovenia, spendidly
illustrated and sumptuously produced.

514 **Art treasures of Slovenia.**
Lev Menaše.   Belgrade: Jugoslovenska revija, 1981. 205p.
An illustrated guide to the contents of the churches and museums of Slovenia by a
leading commentator on the arts.

515 **The Virgin Mary in Slovenian art: the iconography of Marian art
in Slovenia from its beginning to the First World War.**
Lev Menaše, translated by Dusan Gabrovšek.   Celje, Slovenia:
Mohorjeva družba, 1994. 24p.
One of the most characteristic things about the Slovenian landscape is the number of
Baroque churches that dot the hills and valleys across the country. The interiors of
these churches inevitably contain Marian art in the form of small devotional pictures,
frescos and statues. Menaše here discusses the role that this art had in the cultural and
religious life of the Slovenes.

516 **Neue Slovenische Kunst and new Slovenian art.**
Mojca Oblak.   *Art and Design Magazine*, vol. 9, nos. 3/4 (1994),
p. 8-17.
In this special issue of the journal devoted to 'New art from Eastern Europe', Oblak
looks at the radical art group NSK, whose theories 'open a series of paradoxes' (p. 9),
in that they mix established art themes, such as the kitsch art of the Titoist period with
'totalitarian' themes. The article includes 12 full-colour photographs of the work of
Boris Gorenec, Marjelič Potrč, VSSD, Marko Takse, Emerik Bernard. Oblak also
assesses the impact of Irwin's 1991 exhibition *Slovenian Athens*. In the same issue,
Slavoj Žižek discusses 'The Enlightenment in Laibach' (p. 80-7), focusing on visual
images produced by the well-known rock group.

517 **Reisen nach Italien, Tagebuecher, Briefe, Zeichnungen, Aquarelle.**
(Travels to Italy: diaries, letters, drawings and watercolours.)
Karl Friedrich Schinkel, edited by G. Riemann.   Berlin: Ruetten und
Loening, 1979. 359p.

These are the illustrations and German text of the famous Berlin architect's travels across the Slovene lands towards Istria in 1806. Beautifully reproduced in this edition, they show Schinkel's drawing skills particularly well.

518 **Anton Cebej 1722-74.**
Ferdinand Serbelj.   Ljubljana: Narodna galerija, 1991. 209p.

An illustrated catalogue of 64 *opera* by the Baroque painter Anton Cebej, whose work, particularly his frescos, was influenced both by contemporary Italian and Central European trends. His work can be found in Ljubljana and Zagreb as well as Primorska (the Adriatic littoral). The historical text is in English, Italian and Slovene, but the annotated catalogue (p. 73-111) is exclusively in Slovene.

519 **Slovene Impressionists.**
Compiled by France Stele, translated by Elza Jereb, Alasdair
Mackinnon.   St. Paul, Minnesota: Control Data Arts, 1980. 202p.
(1st US ed.).

The Slovene Impressionists Rihard Jakopič, Ivan Grohar and Matija Jama, as well as other less well-known painters who drew their inspiration from the larger continental movement of Impressionism and then created something distinctively Slovene particularly with their landscape portraits, are considered here. The work contains many coloured illustrations and lovers of the Slovenian countryside will appreciate these interpretations of familiar scenes.

520 **France Slana. Watercolours.**
Nace Šumi.   London, New York: Alpine Fine Art Collection, 1987.
200p.

France Slana's delicate style earned this Slovene artist international recognition, particularly in the the United States. See also Janez Mesenel, *France Slana: watercolors, paintings and drawings, 1944-1980* (Minneapolis: Control Data Arts, 1981. 133p.).

521 **Tisnikar – painter of death.**
Nebojša Tomašević.   London: Summerfield Press, 1978. 208p.

Dark gloomy interiors and studies of the grim realities of peasant life reminiscent of the work of Marc Chagall are the subject of this critique of Tisnikar by one of Yugoslavia's foremost art critics and writers.

522 **Sculptor France Gorse.**
R. Večerin in cooperation with John A. Arnez.   New York,
Washington: Studia Slovenica, 1971. 96p.

France Gorse's sculpture drew on traditional Slovene folk motifs, while using innovatory materials and interesting juxtapositions of these with more modern themes.

This illustrated study of his work places him within a Slovene tradition, while also emphasizing the more general accessibility of his work.

523 **Maestri europei dalle collezioni slovene.** (European masters in Slovene collections.)
Edited by Frederico Zeri, Ksenija Rožman. Ljubljana: Narodna galerija, 1993. 202p.

The catalogue of an exhibition held in the spring and summer of 1992 at the National Gallery in Ljubljana to celebrate European paintings in that city. The text is in Italian and Slovene and the work includes a bibliography, index of artists, and many coloured illustrations.

Music and dance

524 **Pipe organs in Slovenia.**
Mirko Bizjak, Edo Škulj. Ljubljana: Državna založba Slovenije, 1985. 232p.

A large-format book with full-colour photographs, this work examines the pipe'organs in Slovenia. These are to be found in Baroque churches, particularly in the Alpine region.

525 **A programme of Renaissance and Baroque music by the Slovene composers Jacobus Gallus and Johannes Baptista Dolar.**
Paul F. Cutter. *Florida State University Slavic Papers*, vol. 1 (1967), p. 100-5.

This paper provided a commentary for a radio broadcast of sixteenth- and seventeenth-century music by composers of Slovene origin in Tallahassee, Florida in 1967. Cutter also gives biographical details of the composers.

526 **Jacobus Gallus Carniolus and his music.**
Dragotin Cvetko. *Slavonic and East European Review*, vol. 31, no. 77 (1953), p. 495-502.

Jacobus Gallus Carniolus (1550-91) is the most influential of all Slovene composers and here Cvetko assesses his life in the sixteenth-century Habsburg monarchy, as well as his musical development. See also Paul F. Cutter, 'Notes on the secular music of Jacobus Gallus', *Papers in Slovene Studies* (1976), p. 179-205.

527 **The Renaissance in Slovene music.**
Dragotin Cvetko. *Slavonic and East European Review*, vol. 36, no. 86 (1957), p. 27-37.

For music to flourish, according to Cvetko, there must not only be the necessary talent but also the right socio-economic conditions. The result of the end of Protestantism in

Slovenia was (very crudely) the increase in Italian cultural influences and the increase in Renaissance music, especially in the late sixteenth and seventeenth centuries. The bishop of Ljubljana, Thomas Hren (1560-1630), is seen as an important cultural influence, along with Ljubljana Cathedral, the Jesuits and the Collegium Marianum. Active musicians of this time included Jacobus Gallus and Janez Krstnik Dolar who taught at the Jesuit college in Ljubljana from 1645 to 1658. His work was published as the collection *Musicalia varia* in 1665. See also Cvetko's 'The problem of national style in South Slavonic music', *Slavonic and East European* Review, vol. 34, no. 82 (1955), p. 1-10.

528   **Jacobus Gallus and his time.**
       Edited by Dragotin Cvetko, Danilo Pokorn.   Ljubljana: Slovenska akademija znanosti in umetnosti, 1986. 168p.
Issued as part of European Music Year this joint English and German text celebrates the work of Slovenia's most famous musician. There are also summaries in Slovene.

529   **Med godci in glasbili na Slovenskem.** (Between musicians and musical instruments in the Slovene lands.)
       Igor Cvetko.   Ljubljana: 1991. 141p.
An illustrated historical survey of music and musicians in Slovenia, which assesses the state of music in the republic after independence. The text is in English and Slovene. Of related interest is his 'The instrumental musical creativity of children in Slovenia', *Studia Instrumentorum Musicae Popularis*, vol. 8 (1985), p. 38-42.

530   **The Slovene Philharmonic and its predecessors.**
       Ivan Klemenčič.   Ljubljana: Slovenska filharmonija, 1988. 178p.
The Philharmonic, one of Ljubljana's two full-size orchestras, still occupies its eighteenth-century Baroque site in Trg Republike, but now performs principally at Cankarjev dom, the purpose-built multi-stage arts centre in Ljubljana. This illustrated history of the orchestra emphasizes the formal musical tradition in Slovenia from the Habsburg period and the involvement of Gustav Mahler in the nineteenth century. The text is in Slovene and English.

531   **The image of war in the Slovene soldierly folk songs: eight centuries in the Habsburg service.**
       Anton Kovač.   *Muenchner Zeitschrift fuer Balkankunde*, vol. 5 (1983/4), p. 17-49.
Examines some of the folk songs referring to war in Karel Štrukelj's collection, *Slovenske narodne pesmi* (Slovene national songs/poems) (Ljubljana: Slovenska matica, 1895-1923, 16 vols). He argues that Slovene peasant culture maintained its autonomy and norms, despite 100 years of incorporation into foreign armies.

532 **Die Volksmusikinstrumente in Slowenien.** (Folk music intruments in Slovenia.)

Zmaga Kumer. Ljubljana: Slovenska akademija znanosti in umetnosti, 1986. 107p.

An examination of some of the traditional folk instruments of Slovenia, including the *citira* (folk violin), the *bunkula* (small three-stringed bass) and the *oprekelj* (dulcimer).

533 **Selected themes of Slovene folk ballads.**

Lena M. Lenček. *Papers in Slovene Studies* (1976), p. 56-89.

Although the Slovenes do not have as rich an oral tradition as their southern neighbours there nevertheless exist recurrent themes in popular folk ballads which are assessed here by Lenček. In the same volume, Rado L. Lenček looks at 'A new version of the ballad *"Kralj Matjaž rescues his captive wife"* in Badouin de Courtenay's collections', *Papers in Slovene Studies* (1976), p. 90-8.

534 **The rock scene in Yugoslavia.**

Pedro Ramet. *East European Politics and Societies*, vol. 2, no. 2 (Spring 1988), p. 396-410.

In his article based on interviews with rock musicians, Ramet considers the sociological significance of the alternative scene, quoting passages of the lyrics of bands such as Lačni Frank (Hungry Frank) from Maribor. A large number of rock groups existed in Slovenia in the 1980s, due to 'liberal political and social attitudes' (p. 399), including the well-known Borghesia and Laibach, which have a large following outside the former Yugoslavia. In considering the fact that Laibach and other groups used controversial Nazi imagery, Ramet quotes the musical director of Ljubljana's Radio Študent, Igor Vidmar: 'In every situation where there are new ideas coming forward, the regime tries to associate them with fascism – which is a totally psychotic reaction. It's the response of dinosaurs'.

535 **Twentieth century Slovene composers.**

Andrej Rijavec. Ljubljana: Društvo slovenskih skladateljev; Cologne: Musikverlag H. Gerig, 1975. 96p.

Assesses the work of the modern Slovene composers Marij Kogoj, Slavko Osterc and Lucijan Skerjanec.

Theatre and film

536 **In the depths.**

France Berk. *Slavonic and East European Review*, vol. 15, no. 43 (July 1936), p. 14-29.

A one-act play in the form of dialogues between soldiers in a dug-out who are eventually killed by the explosion of a hand-grenade.

537 **Tomorrow.**
Evald Fliser, with a commentary by Leigh Johnson.   London:
Goldhawk Press, in association with Ganes, Ljubljana, 1992. 76p.
Set in Siberia, the play is based on conversations about the meaning of existence
between its four characters: Rembrandt, Yessenin, Nijinski and Mishkin. A radio
version of the play was first broadcast on BBC Radio 3 on 31 August 1980. It has
subsequently been performed in Ljubljana and the edition also includes a parallel
Slovene text *Jutri bo lepše* (Tomorrow will be more beautiful).

538 **What about Leonardo?**
Evald Fliser, with a commentary by Leigh Johnson.   London:
Goldhawk Press, in association with Ganes, Ljubljana, 1992. 101p.
Set in a neurological institute, the inflexible Dr DaSilva 'represents the relentless
pursuer of change in the human psyche' (p. 99) whereas her male colleague Dr
Hoffman needs to care and nurture. A humorous play with a dark twist. A parallel
Slovene text *Kaj pa Leonardo?* is also published in this edition.

539 **Ksenija Mišič.**
Bojana Leskovar, with photographs by Angelo Božac.   *Ars Vivendi*,
no. 16 (Dec. 1992), p. 70-7.
Interview with one of the leading actresses of the younger generation in Maribor in a
magazine devoted to promoting Slovenian arts.

540 **On the exceptional upswing of dramatic writing in Slovenia.**
Tone Peršak.   *Le Livre Slovène*, vol. 21, nos. 1/2 (1983), p. 62-7.
Covers the rise of avant-garde theatre in Ljubljana and Maribor in the 1980s as the politi-
cal atmosphere became more relaxed after a relatively quiet period in the mid-1970s.

541 **Slovenian cinema in post-war Yugoslavia.**
Ljubljana: Zveza kulturinih organizacij Slovenije, 1983. 103p.
The Slovenian film-makers František Cap, Franci Slak, Filip Robar and Boštjan
Hladnik, amongst others, are little known outside Slovenia, although their work has
often appeared at international film festivals. This short introduction to post-war film
in Slovenia introduces the often avant-garde and experimental work of these artists,
whose work is frequently considered to be esoteric by the Slovenian public, who
generally prefer the more pedestrian themes of American films. The text is in Slovene
and English.

542 **Antigone.**
Dominik Smole, translated by Harry Leeming.   Murska sobota,
Slovenia: Pomorski tisk, Ljubljana, 1988 for Mladinska knjiga
International. 68p.
A modern version of an ancient tragedy, considered to be one of the best plays of the
post-war era. Although Antigone is never actually present on stage, she is a constant
presence in the speeches of the other protagonists: Ismene, Creon, Haimon and
Teiresias. It was thought to have strong political overtones when it was performed by
the Oder 57 theatre group active in Ljubljana between 1957 and 1964.

Folklore

543 **Kresnik-Krstnik, ein Wesen aus der kroatischen und slowenischen Volksueberlieferung.** (Kresnik-Krstnik, a being in Croat and Slovene popular tradition.)
Maja Bošković-Stulli. *Fabula*, vol. 3, no. 3 (1959-60), p. 275-98.

A seminal article on the *Kresnik*, a figure with supposed mystical powers, that has influenced other Central European writers.

544 **Rituals and customs along the Kolpa (Bela krajina).**
Joseph L. Conrad. *Slovene Studies*, vol. 7, nos. 1-2 (1985), p. 23-33.

The folklore of the Bela krajina area, particularly that associated with the seasons of year, is outlined in this article. The rituals associated with Christmas, St John's Day and St George's Day are explained in some detail through interviews with local people and the use of Slovene-language secondary sources. Conrad argues that the beliefs in this area have parallels with other South Slavic cultures and this is in part because of the population movement northwards that followed the Turkish expansion in the Balkans.

545 **Slovene oral incantations: topics, text and ritual.**
Joseph L. Conrad. *Slovene Studies*, vol. 12, no. 1 (1990), p. 55-66.

Oral incantations (*zagovori*) have survived across the Slovene-speaking areas into the twentieth century. As Conrad argues, incantations may generally fall into three categories to alleviate either external physical injuries, internal ailments or social relations. Over 500 varieties of vegetation are known in Slovene folk medicine as salves. It is generally held that incantations are pre-Christian, including those to banish the 'Evil Eye', but that they now have a Christian veneer, particularly in the invocation of particular saints.

546 **Slovene folklore.**
Fanny S. Copeland. *Folklore*, vol. 42 (1931), p. 405-46.

Copeland outlines some of the main themes of Slovene folklore, particularly in the Alpine region. See also her 'Some aspects of Slovene folklore', *Folklore*, vol. 60 (1949), p. 277-86.

547 **Slovene myths.**
Fanny S. Copeland. *Slavonic Review*, vol. 11, no. 33 (April 1933), p. 631-58.

A full-length review of the work of Jakob Kelemina, whose book *Bajke in pripovedke slovenskega ljudsva* (Popular myths and folktales of the Slovene people) was published in 1930. The article includes Copeland's own comparisons of Slovene myths with those of other European countries. There are also translations of the legends of *Zlatorog* (The Golden Horn) and the Tenth Sister.

548 **Lampret, the warlock marksman.**
Fanny S. Copeland. *Slavonic Review*, vol. 13, no. 37 (July 1934), p. 20-6.

A traditional folktale about a hunter with magic bullets, adapted from the Slovene version given by Jakob Kelemina, a leading authority on popular culture. For a regional perspective of the south-west of Slovenia, see Francis J. Kess, 'Ribnica tales among the American Slovenians', *Journal of the Ohio Folklore Society*, vol. 4 (1968), p. 201-10.

549 **The golden bird. Folk tales from Slovenia.**
Edited by Vladimir Kavčič, translated by J. Dekker, Lena M. Lenček. Cleveland, Ohio; New York: World Paper Company, 1969. 217p.

For a comparison see also *How the sun was brought back to the sky* written by Mirra Ginsburg and with pictures by Jože Aruego and Ariadne Dewey (New York: Macmillan, 1975. 32p.), which was adapted from a Slovenian folktale.

550 **The concept of folklore in Yugoslavia.**
Milko Matičetov. *Journal of the Folklore Institute*, vol. 3 (1966), p. 398-418.

A historical survey of the study of folklore in Yugoslavia by one of Slovenia's leading collectors of folklore. Matičetov is probably best known for his empirical work on the Karst and the valley of Resia in north-east Italy, on which he is an unrivalled source of knowledge.

551 **Possibilities of psychological interpretations of the literary folklore.**
Marija Stanovnik. *Narodna umjetnost*, vol. 30 (1992), p. 157-65.

Traces the (mostly indirect) influence of Jung in Slovene and European folklore studies. In the case of the Slovenes, the work of Anton Trstenjak and Ivan Prijatelj, who published *Psihologični paralelizem* (Psychological parallelism) in 1902 is particularly significant.

Festivals, customs, costumes and ethnographic studies

552 **Bee-hive art.**
Kalami Adanja. *Review* (Belgrade), (June 1967), p. 21-8.

The painted panels on the ends of bee-hives (*panjska končnica*) were the little miracle of Slovene peasant art, particularly in the nineteenth century. They depicted everything from farmers ploughing to the devil or festival dances. For a discussion of the content of this art see also Niko Kuret, 'Das Volksschauspiel in der Volkskunst der Slovenen' (Dramatic scenes in the popular art of the Slovenes), *Etnologica*

Slavica, vols. 8-9 (1976-77), p. 271-81, which includes black-and-white illustrations of the bee-hive paintings.

553 Rise from want: a peasant family in the machine age.

James C. Davis. Philadelphia: University of Philadelphia Press, 1986. 165p. maps. bibliog.

Traces the fortunes of a single Slovene family, the Žužeks from the village of Duino (Sl. Devin) in north-east Italy, from the earliest extant documents in the sixteenth century. The narrative of the family's life is placed in the context of the modernization and industrialization of this part of the Adriatic coastline, particularly since the late eighteenth century.

554 Oryctographia Carniolica oder physicalische Erdbeschreibung des Herzogthums Krain, Istrien und zum Theil der benachtbarten Laender. (Physical description of the lands of the Duchy of Carniola, Istria and parts of the neighbouring areas.)

Balthasar Hacquet. Leipzig: Johann Gottlob Immanuel Breitkopf, 1778-89. 4 vols.

An ethnological and physical description of Slovene and Croatian ethnic areas by the eminent writer and traveller Balthasar Hacquet. See also *Hacquets mineralogisch-botanische Lustreise von dem Berg Terglou in Krain zu dem Berg Glockner in Tyrol im Jahr 1779 und 81* (Hacquet's mineralogical and botanical travels from Mount Triglav in Carniola to Glockner in the Tyrol in the years 1779 and 1781) (Vienna: Johann Paul Krausischen Buchhandlung, 1784. 149p.).

555 Suburban villagers: a Slovenian case study.

Slavko Kremenšek, translated by Vilko Novak, edited by Joel M. Halpern. Amherst, Massachusetts: University of Massachusetts, Dept of Anthropology, 1979. 53p. (Program in Soviet and East European Studies, no. 2).

A study of the village of Moste near Ljubljana, which gradually became part of the town itself during the nineteenth century. Kremenšek, a leading Slovenian ethnologist, assesses the effect of industrialization on a 'traditional' economy. See also his 'Ethnology of Ljubljana: an element of the research project "the way of life of Slovenes in the twentieth century"', *Urban Anthropology*, vol. 13 (1984), p. 309-27.

556 Masken der Slowenen. (Masks of the Slovenes.)

Niko Kuret. *Schweizerisches Archiv fuer Volkskunde*, vol. 63, nos. 3/4 (1967), p. 203-25.

Kuret, a leading Slovene ethnologist who died in 1995, was responsible for much of the study of traditional festivals such as Pustni torek (Shrove Tuesday) in Ptuj. Here he outlines some of the main characteristics of the masks of the Slovenes, including the winter masks used in the above festival. Kuret's main work *Praznično leto Slovencev* (The festival year of the Slovenes) (Celje, Slovenia: Mohorjeva družba, 1967. 2 vols), although unfortunately not available in English, is one of the major studies of Slovene popular culture.

557 **The homemade world of Zagaj: an interpretation of the practical life among traditional peasant-farmers in West-Haloze, Slovenia.**
Robert Gary Minnich.   Bergen, Norway: Sosialantropologisk Institut, 1979. 248p. maps.

This short study of *furež* (the killing and subsequent preparation of pork products) in the Haloze region just south of Ptuj and close to the Croatian border is an anthropological classic and deserves to be widely known beyond the field of Slovene studies. Beginning with a historical discussion of the peasantry in Haloze, Minnich presents his own field research done while living in Zagaj in the 1970s. Of particular interest are the photographs that accompany the text; these include one of a child happily playing with a severed pig's head. This book is enough to turn any 'townie' into a vegetarian.

558 **The symbolic dimension of West Haloze peasant technology.**
Robert Minnich.   *Slovene Studies*, vol. 4, no. 1 (1982), p. 21-7.

Considers the symbolic place of *furež* (pig-sticking) in West Haloze. Paraphrasing Clifford Geertz, when writing about cock-fighting in Bali, Minnich feels that 'pigsticking becomes for Haložani a story about themselves which they tell themselves' (p. 25). In the naive art of the former Yugoslavia, pig-sticking occurs as a motif more often than the rituals concerning death, baptism or folk-healing. All elements of peasant life are encapsulated in this ritual: the division of labour along gendered lines, balanced reciprocity between farmsteads and the feast.

559 **Tradition in the face of modernisation: cultural continuity and 'deagrarisation' in the village of Ukve.**
Robert Minnich.   *Slovene Studies*, vol. 11, nos. 1-2 (1989), p. 97-108.

Ukve is situated in the Val Canale in north-east Italy and is of interest, argues Minnich, because of the persistence of traditional economic practices such as transhumance.

560 **The gift of 'koline' and the articulation of identity in Slovene peasant society.**
Robert G. Minnich.   *Etnologia Slavica*, vol. 22 (1990), p. 151-61.

Koline in Slovene means the household products of butchering, which tend to be exchanged between close family relations as gifts. When sold at the market for cash, other words such as *svinja* (pork) are used. Gift exchange is primarily associated with acephalous (clan-based) societies and commodity exchange with a state or class society. Household production of pork was unusually large in the former Yugoslavia, accounting for 60 per cent of pigs slaughtered in 1985. Pig husbandry has been important in the Slovene lands since at least the sixteenth century. Minnich then proceeds to discuss the links between *koline* and *furež* (pig-sticking) in Haloze.

561 **Arhitektura slovenskega kozolca / Architecture of the Slovene 'kozolec'.**
Marjan Mušič.   Ljubljana: Cankarjeva založba, 1970. 165p.

The hayrack is one of the most characteristic parts of the agricultural landscape in Slovenia. Designed to dry hay quickly because of erratic weather conditions, the design is also found in Scandinavia. See also Jaka Čop and Tone Cevc, translated by

Irena Šumi and Victoria Rashke, *Slovenski kozolec / Slovene hay rack* (Žirovnica: Agens, 1993. 240p.), which also has a parallel Slovene and English text.

562 Slovenian ethnology between the past and the present.

Ingrid Slavec. *Etnologia Slavica*, vol. 22 (1990), p. 217-42.

Discusses the history of Slovenian ethnology, since the early modern period, but focuses on the institutionalization of the subject in the twentieth century, particularly the foundation of the Ethnographic Museum in 1923, the journal *Etnolog* (1926-44), and its successor *Slovenski Etnograf* (1948-) and the first appearance of *Glasnik* in 1956. As Slavec writes, 'the best illustration of pre-war ethnology is certainly the synthetic anthology *Narodopisje Slovencev* (1944-52) (The ethnology of the Slovenes) [which] at the level permitted by a positively orientated cultural-historical study, [it] presents ethnology as a science which is concerned with the various elements of . . . peasant culture, its sources and diffusions, to some extent also its changes' (p. 220). As she argues, increasingly since the war the scope and methods of ethnology have been questioned. Should folk culture be the main object of study? What should the relationship be between ethnology and other disciplines? Slavec then discusses the progress of the Slovenian ethnological bibliography and the role of practical work in museums. A version of this paper also appeared in *Etnološki pregled*, nos. 23-4 (1988), p. 37-59.

563 The anthropological tradition in Slovenia.

Zmago Šmitek, Božidar Jezernik. In: *Fieldwork and footnotes: studies in the history of European anthropology.* Edited by Han F. Vermeulen, Arturo Alvarez Roldan. London: Routledge, 1995, p. 171-83.

The authors argue that a fundamental distinction should be made between 'anthropology', which has been formally institutionalized at the Faculty of Philosophy at Ljubljana University only since 1991 and 'ethnology' which is more established. Whereas anthropology is a holistic science, which concerns itself with such questions as the difference between humans and animals, ethnology has largely been preoccupied with the folk customs of the Slovenes and it is therefore to be considered as an essentially 'national' discipline. There are several pre-twentieth-century Slovenes whom the authors consider to have 'anthropological' concerns in their work, including Benedikt Kupripečič, who wrote the oldest known traveller's account of the Balkans in 1531 and Friderik Baraga, who published a study of native Americans in 1837.

564 Bobbin lace: a cottage industry.

Jelka Urh. *CIBA Review*, no. 1 (1966), p. 31-40.

A special issue of *CIBA Review*, published by the Ciba Foundation in Basel. It is dedicated to Slovene textiles, and includes the article 'Bela krajina textiles' by Bozo Račič (p. 18-23), and 'Sieve-weaving in Stražišče' by W. F. Schweizer (p. 24-30). Jelka Urh examines the history of lace-making (*čipka*) in Idrija. The entire volume is beautifully illustrated with full-colour photographs of textiles, frescos and machines.

565   **A Slovenian village: Žerovnica.**
Irene Portis Winner.   Providence, Rhode Island: Brown University
Press, 1971. 276p. maps. bibliog.

Probably the most widely accessible account of the Karst area of Slovenia, which
brilliantly reproduces village life in Žerovnica. It was written by an American
anthropologist, who lived in a village on the banks of Lake Cerknica for a year. She
set out to show how Žerovnica was a 'typical Slovenian village' (p. 4). The result is a
highly readable account of daily life in a Slovene village in the late 1960s. It is
crammed with meticulous details from contemporary observations about the family,
occupations, diet, houses, fields, land-holding, and farming techniques. It has been
called a 'model study' by James C. Davis.

566   **The question of the *zadruga* in Slovenia. Myth and reality in
Žerovnica.**
Irene Portis Winner.   *Anthropological Quarterly*, vol. 50, no. 2
(1977), p. 125-34.

The *zadruga* or communal farm, which existed across South Slav ethnic territory until
the beginning of this century, was not known amongst the Slovenes. In this article, the
American anthropologist questions why this form was absent in Slovenia.

Food and Drink

567 **Slovenska kuharica.** (Slovene cuisine.)
Felicita Kalinšek.   Ljubljana: Cankarjeva žalozba, 1990. 712p.
A vast compendium of Slovene recipes, including *Prekmurska gibanica*, a dessert from the eastern part of the country.

568 **Kuharstvo.** (Cuisine.)
Pepika Levstik.   Ljubljana: Državna založba Slovenije, 1994. 3rd ed. 498p.
Slovene cuisine varies greatly between regions: goose with red cabbage is standard fare in Ptuj, blood sausages in Bled and mussels in thick sauce in Istria. This standard reference work gives the interested reader a glimpse of the Slovenian culinary repertoire.

569 **Slovenska kuharica ali navod okusno kuhati navadna in imenitna jedila.** (Slovene cuisine: guide to delicious cookery for everyday and special occasions.)
Magadalena Pleiweis.   Ljubljana: Ara, 1994. 320p.
Guide to Slovene-style entertainment, including *potica*, a walnut roll speciality.

Libraries, Art Galleries, Museums and Archives

570 **Guide to the university libraries of the work community Alps-Adria.**
Edited by Srečko Jelušič.   Rijeka, Slovenia: Vladimir Bakarič University Press, 1988. 141p.

Brief guide to the history, contents and staff of the university libraries of Maribor and Ljubljana, as well as other equivalent libraries within the Alpe-Adria working group at that time (i.e., Austria, Germany, Italy and Croatia).

571 **The architecture museum: reclaiming Slovenia's heritage.**
Peter Krečič, translated by Ljubica Klančar, Toby Robertson. Ljubljana: Architectural Museum, Lucas, 1994. 20p.

A brief illustrated guide to Ljubljana's Architecture Museum, which covers a vast range of architectural styles from medieval to contemporary.

572 **A guide to the museums of Slovenia.**
Edited by Gregor Moder, with an introduction by Ralf Čeplak, translated by Roger Metcalfe, Mika Briški.   Ljubljana: Association of Museums of Slovenia, 1993. 126p.

Since the beginning of the decade a great deal of attention has been paid to the restoration of museums, including Ljubljanski grad and smaller provincial museums in Ptuj, in the Alps, and on the coastline. Slovenia's cultural heritage is very varied and conscientiously preserved and this guide would be particularly useful to those travelling outside the capital. For a guide to Slovenia's seventeenth- and eighteenth-century monuments, see Nace Šumi, *The Baroque monuments of Slovenia* (Ljubljana: Zavod Republike Slovenije za varstvo, naravne in kulturne dediščine. 1992. 117p.).

573 **COBISS – A cooperative online bibliographic system and services in Slovenia.**
T. Seljak. *Program-automated Library and Information Systems*, vol. 28, no. 3 (1994), p. 287-93.

Outlines the progress to date in automating the National Library (NUK) and other smaller libraries throughout the republic.

574 **Slovenski etnografski muzej / The Slovenian ethnographic museum.**
Bojana Rogelj Skafar, translated by Franc Smrk, Jean McCollister.
Ljubljana: Etnografski muzej, Gorenski tisk, Kranj, 1993. 93p.

Issued to celebrate its 70th anniversary in 1993, this sumptuously produced full-colour guide to the museum collection includes a catalogue of 59 objects, which include a wooden plough (p. 29), a dormouse trap (p. 37) and a wooden dumpling ladle (p. 87). The full text appears in English, French and Slovene.

575 **Naravna in kulturna dediščina slovenskega naroda / Investigations into the natural and cultural heritage of the Slovene nation.**
Edited by Majda Stanonik-Blinc. Ljubljana: Slovenska akademija znanosti in umetnosti, 1988. 96p.

This bilingual guide to the research institutes within the Slovenian Academy includes a brief chronology of the institutes, executive officers, academic members of staff, and outlines of their research programmes.

Publishing and Mass Media

Books, newspapers and periodicals

576 **The novelty of** *Nova revija.*
Lev Deleta.   *South Slav Journal*, vol. 5, no. 3 (Autumn 1982),
p. 37-40.

Nova revija was founded in 1982 as a liberal cultural journal after two years of discussion between Dimitrij Rupel, Taras Kermauner, Dušan Jovanović and other radicals of the younger generation. As the editor Tine Hribar wrote in the second issue, 'We are returning to where we were 20 years ago. As at the beginning of the 1960s, signs of a more liberal and elastic cultural life are reappearing. The ideological repression which submerged us in the mid-1970s has led to economic as well as new cultural policies' (p. 39-40).

577 **Slovenian books.**
Editor-in-chief Branko Hofman.   Ljubljana: Mladinska knjiga; Koper:
Založba Lipa, 1987. 132p.

Reviews books available in English about Slovenia, as well as serving as an introduction to Slovenia's publishing houses and a short guide to book production in Slovenia.

578 **The development of Slovene and Yugoslav periodical journalism.**
Fran Vatovec.   Ljubljana: Visoka šola za politične vede, 1968. 106p.

Historical survey of periodical journalism in the former Yugoslavia, concentrating on Slovenia.

Radio and television

579 **The TV scenic designs of Jože Spačal.**
Stane Bernik, foreword by Nace Šumi and Jure Mikuž, translated by
Milan Mlačnik, Mark Valentine. Ljubljana: Tiskana Delo, 1993.
[n.p.].
This was printed on the occasion of a retrospective art exhibition in Ljubljana in 1993.
Spačal has left his imprint on contemporary art both as a mosaicist, and as the
designer of over 300 sets for Slovenian television.

580 **Slovenia for everyone.**
Edited by Tomaž Gerdina, Government Public Relations and Media
Office, Amidas and Atlantic. Ljubljana: Vitrium, 1994. 95p. maps.
Comprehensive guide to public facilities in the republic.

581 **The media and the war.**
Marina Gržinić. *Art and Design Magazine*, vol. 9, nos. 3/4 (1994),
p. 18-25.
Gržinić, a Croatian video artist living in Ljubljana, describes her 'vigil' besides the
television during the war in Slovenia and the impact of the war on her own work.

582 **Slovenian Media Guide '94.**
Janja Božič Marolt. Mediana Research Institute, Ljubljana published
by Primožič, Kranj, 1994. 160p.
Comprehensive guide to the media in Slovenia, including detailed profiles of the
television and radio stations as well as details of the larger magazines and newpapers.
It does not include academic publications and aims to profile what are assumed to be
the mainstream interests. The average Slovene adult is reported to spend over 250
minutes daily listening to the radio, while over fifty per cent of the readership of
Kmečki glas (Peasant Voice) is 40 years of age or older. Overall, a good guide for the
sociologist to the vivacity of the Slovenian media, and an invaluable piece of market
research for anyone planning to invest in Slovenia. The country profile (p. 1-5)
includes brief statistics on population, higher education and the economy.

583 **The role of television in a period of ethnic tensions.**
Nenad Pejić. London: Wyndham Place Trust R. K. Hudson, 1992.
24p. (Corbishley Memorial Lecture, no. 16).
Looks at the role of the media during the initial stages of the wars in former
Yugoslavia, including that in Slovenia.

Professional Periodicals

584 **Ars Vivendi.**
Ljubljana: DOMUS, 1988- . quarterly.
Art and fashion periodical, published quarterly in both Slovene- and English-language editions by DOMUS in Ljubljana.

585 **Flaneur.**
Ljubljana: Vitrium, January 1992- . monthly.
Monthly ecological magazine with full-colour photographs and English text.

586 **IN: Information from Slovenia.**
Ljubljana: International Press Center, April 1990- . weekly.
A weekly broadsheet that covers political and financial as well as cultural information published by the Ljubljana International Press Center, Poljanska 31, Ljubljana, Republic of Slovenia.

587 **Marketing Magazine.**
Ljubljana: Tiskana Delo, 1981- . irregularly.
Published irregularly from 1981 onwards, *Marketing Magazine* presents the world of Slovenian business to the English-language reader. Of particular interest is the July 1991 issue (no. 123), celebrating 'Europe's youngest state', which is a good guide to the best of Slovenian business and culture.

588 **Papers in Slovene Studies.**
New York: Society for Slovene Studies, 1975-78. annual.
The forerunner to *Slovene Studies*, published in annual book form by the Society for Slovene Studies.

589 Slovene Studies.
New York: Society for Slovene Studies, 1979- . twice per year.

The journal of the Society for Slovene Studies, which publishes two volumes a year. The major English-language source on all matters relating to Slovenia and to Slovenes outside Slovenia. An indispensable and meticulously edited source for scholarship, which includes book reviews (of Slovene-language material), articles in English with Slovene summaries, conference reports, and review articles.

590 Slovenian Business Report.
Ljubljana: Gospodarski vestnik, January 1993- . monthly.

Published by Gospodarski vestnik and printed by Delo in Ljubljana, this monthly guide to business is an invaluable English-language source for statistical, legal and other data relating to the Republic of Slovenia.

591 Slovenija: The Slovenian Newsletter.
London: Betts/Valenčič, June 1991- . 3 or 4 issues per year.

Founded in immediate response to the crisis in Slovenia in the summer of 1991 by the main editor Jana Valenčič and Michael Betts, the newsletter acts as an informative broadsheet that brings together the Slovene community in Britain. Published 3 to 4 times a year by Betts/Valenčič, 12 Flitcroft Street, London WC2 8DJ.

592 The South Slav Journal.
London: Dositey Obradovich Circle, 1978- . irregular.

Published by the Dositey Obradovich Circle in London, this journal has acted since its foundation as a monitor of political developments in the former Yugoslavia. It publishes interviews with politicians, political manifestos and other articles of a contemporary and historical nature, often with a distinctly *emigré* flavour.

Encyclopedia

593 **Enciklopedija Slovenije.**
Ljubljana: Mladinska knjiga, 1987. maps.

Eight volumes of this comprehensive illustrated encyclopaedia had been produced by 1994. Another four volumes are projected.

Bibliographies

594 The economic history of Slovenia 1828-1918.
Toussaint Hočevar. New York: Society for Slovene Studies, 1978. 50p.

Lists 234 books and articles on the Slovenian economy during the early stages of industrialization. Slovene titles have been translated into English.

595 A tentative bibliography on Slovene proverbs.
Anthony J. Klančar. *Journal of American Folklore*, vol. 61 (1948), p. 194-200.

Anthony Klančar was a very active promoter of matters Slovene after the Second World War. Here he collated material relating to proverbs, largely published in German and Slovene.

596 Slovenia: a bibliography in foreign languages.
Valentin Leskovšek. New York; Washington, DC: Studia Slovenica, 1991. 2 vols.

A comprehensive bibliography of materials relating to Slovenia and the Slovenes in languages other than Slovene, but largely in English, German, Italian and French.

597 Resia: bibliografia ragionata 1927-1979. (Resia: a regional bibliography 1927-79.)
Milko Matičetov. Udine: Graphik Studio, 1981. 39p.

A bibliography of the Italian and Slovene-language materials on this small valley near Udine, where an archaic form of Slovene is preserved in the local dialect.

598 **Bibliografia storico-religiosa su Trieste e l'Istria 1864-1974.**
(Historical and religious bibliography on Trieste and Istria
1864-1974.)
P. A. Passolunghi, P. Zovatto. Rome: Multigrafica Editrice, 1978.
188p.

Lists 2201 items concerning the history (mostly religious) of Istria, including areas which now form part of the Republic of Slovenia. The items are arranged chronologically.

599 **Slovenia.**
Carole Rogel. *Canadian Review of Studies in Nationalism*, vol. 9
(1982), p. 101-10.

Rogel, one of the leading authorities on Slovene history in North America, reviews the work of over thirty historical texts about Slovenia and discusses the importance of the historical journal *Zgodovinski Časopis*. She argues that among Slovene historians there was 'a broad consensus that the ethnic community was the proper subject for historical investigation'. She also points out that although social and economic history have dominated the discipline, that their work cannot be characterized as Marxist in a political and ideological sense. The work of Slovenes writing about Italy and Austria is also considered in the final section.

600 **Slovenska bibliografija.** (Slovenian bibliography.)
Ljubljana: Izdala in Založila Narodna in Univerzitetna Knjižnica,
1946- .

Comprehensive bibliography of all material published in the Republic of Slovenia.

601 **American linguists on Slovene language. A comprehensive
annotated bibliography (1940-1975).**
[Society for Slovene Studies]: New York: Society for Slovene Studies,
1975. ix, 19p.

Concerns the highly specialized literature produced by American Slavists on the Slovene language and its fascinating peculiarities.

Indexes

There follow three separate indexes: authors (personal and corporate); titles; and subjects. Title entries are italicized and refer either to the main titles, or to other works cited in the annotations. The numbers refer to bibliographical entry rather than page numbers. Individual index entries are arranged in alphabetical sequence.

Index of Authors

C

Cadell, W. A. 77
Campbell, J. C. 210
Cankar, I. 239, 466, 475-8
Canning, P. 303
Carcas, G. 273
Carmichael, C. 38, 78
Carter, A. 323
Carter, F. W. 37
Čebulj-Sajko, B. 280
Čekuta, V. 203
Čepič, Z. 133
Čerar, M. 344
Čermelj, L. 211-12
Černič, B. 360
Černigoj-Sadar, N. 300, 308
Cevc, T. 561
Chetkovich, Sasha 378
Chetkovich, Sven 378
Christian, H. A. 193
Christian, H. H. 87
Christie, A. 259
Christitch, A. 169
Christitch, E. 3, 281
Churchill, G. C. 80
Cizmič, I. 87
Clissold, J. 170
Cole, M. M. 22
Coley, J. A. 56
Collomb, R. G. 57
Conrad, J. L. 544-5
Cook, A. J. 79
Cooper, H. R. 253, 452-4
Čop, J. 561
Copeland, F. S. 58-9, 546-8
Čopič, M. 387
Cornwall, M. 171
Cox, G. 213
Črnobrnja, M. 322
Croci, O. 226
Crow, J. 325-6
Cuisenier, J. 52
Čuješ, R. 4, 361-2
Čukjati, K. 194
Čuliberg, M 48
Čurčič, B. 103
Cutter, P. F. 525-6
Cvetko, D. 526-8
Cvetko, I. 529
Cvikl, M. 367

D

Dacie, A. 91
Danielis, R. 366
David, Z. V. 129
Davidson, M. 455, 478
Davis, J. C. 214, 388, 553
Davis, M. G. 243
Debeljak, A. 479
Debelkova, M. 59
Dedijer, V. 323
Deeleman-Reinhold, C. L. 104
Dekleva, J. 299
Deleta, L. 576
Derbyshire, W. W. 274
Detoni, M. 119
Devetak, S. 181, 244
Dews, P. 304
Dimitz, A. 134
Dimnik, M. 282-3
Dokič, N. S. 353
Dolence, M. 60
Donchenko, A. K. 287
Drakulić, S. 92
Drnovšek, M. 284
Drobne, K. 39-40
Drofenik, O. 439
Drovenik, M. 41
Drušković, D. 234
Dwyer, J. D. 195
Dyck, R. G. 309

E

Eekman, T. 253, 480
Ellerman, D. P. 379
Englefield, G. 324
Erjavec, A. 172
Evans, R. J. W. 126-7
Eveno, C. 504

F

Fabjan, I. 61
Fajfar, P. 446
Feldstein, R. F. 245
Felicjan, J. 345
Ferenc, T. 156
Ferk, J. 481
Ferligoj, A. 442

Fettich, J. 310
Fischer, J. 389
Fliser, E. 537-8
Frieze, I. H. 442
Friš, D. 284
Froot, K. 365
Fuller, G. J. 22
Furlan, B. 157

G

Gadanyi, K. 262
Galton, H. 246
Gams, I. 42-4
Gantar, M. 106
Ganthar, P. 385
Gelt, D. 135
Genorio, R. 196, 203
Gerdina, T. 580
Gestrin, F. 133, 145
Giarreta, G. 62
Gilbert, J. 80
Ginsburg, M. 549
Glušić, H. 469
Gobetz, E. 5
Gobetz, G. E. 197
Golush, R. A. 245
Good, D. F. 363
Gorup, R. 247
Gosar, A. 62-3
Gosar, P. 447
Gould, S. W. 176
Grad, A. 267-8
Gradišnik, B. 483-4
Grafenauer, B. 133, 215
Grafenauer, N. 354
Granda, S. 380
Gray, C. W. 346
Gray, L. F. 157
Grčević, M. 115
Gross, F. 216
Gruenwald, O. 456
Gržarc-Butina, D. 510
Gržinić, M. 580

H

Habe, F. 64
Hacquet, B. 373, 554
Hafner, D. F. 327
Hajnšek-Holz, M. 265

Index of Titles

163

Index of Subjects

S

Šalamun, Tomaz 499
Salecl, Renata 304
Samorastniki 466, 501
Schinkel, Karl Friedrich 517
scientific research 445-9
self-management 329, 369, 391, 400
Šeligo, Rudi 455
Serb nationalism as a centralizing force in Yugoslavia 337
Serbo-Croat as executive language 257
Situla art 115
Slana, France 520
Slovene as a description 11
Slovene Defence Force 326
Slovene language
general 241-2, 251-3,
accents 254, 260
bilingualism 190, 201, 208-9, 234, 264, 444
dialects 255-6
dual form 55, 248
familiar and formal address 249, 388
history of language 237, 252, 258, 261, 263, 271, 283, 292
neo-circumflex 250
richness of vocabulary 482
stress-shifts 245
Valvasor as a source 261
differences from other languages
English 243, 259
non-Slavonic languages 249
Serbo-Croat 239-40, 242, 247, 249, 262
Slavonic languages 246

Slovene Writers' Society 320
Slovenes in Argentina 194, 196, 284
in Australia 280, 458
in Austria 189, 207-9, 215, 218, 224, 227-8, 234, 256, 440
see also Interallied Plebiscite Commission
in Canada 203, 284-5
in Italy 206, 211-12, 214, 216-18, 220-3, 226, 232, 440, 553, 559
see also Geography: Trieste; History: 'Trieste Question'; Osimo Agreements; 'Race for Trieste'
in the USA
general 73, 87-8, 192-3, 195, 197-200, 204-5, 284
American Slovene language 199
bilingualism 201
newspapers 195
political activity 204
names for Slovenes 202
religious activity 286
translation of names 200
Slovenia as a part of Yugoslavia 165-7, 169, 179, 188, 338
as part of Europe 177, 321, 330, 352, 357
Slovenian independence – its recognition 353, 358
Slovenian War of Independence 318, 338, 354, 581, 584
Slovenska matica 441
Smolnikar Affair 334

Social issues
general 299-301
alcohol consumption 297
childcare provision 300
family life 308, 317
political responses 299
refugees 298, 338
role of women 2, 231, 296, 302, 305, 411
Society for Slovene Studies 589
Soviet Union 95
Stalin, Josef 329
statistics 412-13, 590

T

Tavčar, Ivan 468
Tisnikar, Zoran 521
Tito, Josip Broz 313
tolar 378, 382
tourism 62-3
trade 350, 386, 390
see also international relations; privately owned sector; self-management
trades unions 2
transhumance 22, 27
transport 351, 405-7, 423, 433
Treaty of Paris, February 1947 32
Triglav National Park 23, 56, 61
Trubar, Primož 282-3, 288, 293, 464
Truman, Harry S. 213

U

US policy towards Slovenia 355
unemployment *see* workforce
Uradni list 350
ustoličevanje see Dukes of Carinthania, investiture

175

Map of Slovenia

This map shows the more important towns and other features.

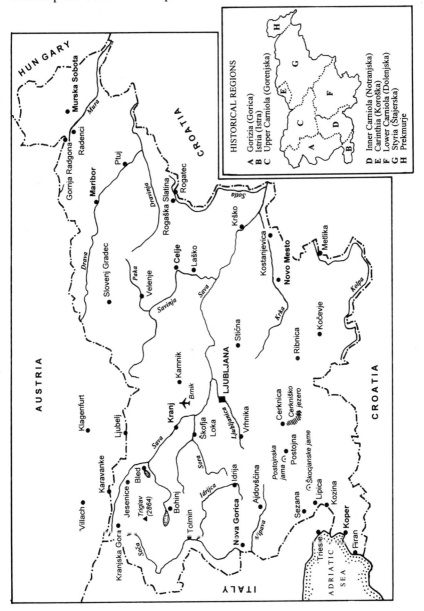

HISTORICAL REGIONS

A Gorizia (Gorica)
B Istria (Istra)
C Upper Carniola (Gorenjska)
D Inner Carniola (Notranjska)
E Carinthia (Koroška)
F Lower Carniola (Dolenjska)
G Styria (Štajerska)
H Prekmurje

ALSO FROM CLIO PRESS

INTERNATIONAL ORGANIZATIONS SERIES

Each volume in the International Organizations Series is either devoted to one specific organization, or to a number of different organizations operating in a particular region, or engaged in a specific field of activity. The scope of the series is wide-ranging and includes intergovernmental organizations, international non-governmental organizations, and national bodies dealing with international issues. The series is aimed mainly at the English-speaker and each volume provides a selective, annotated, critical bibliography of the organization, or organizations, concerned. The bibliographies cover books, articles, pamphlets, directories, databases and theses and, wherever possible, attention is focused on material about the organizations rather than on the organizations' own publications. Notwithstanding this, the most important official publications, and guides to those publications, will be included. The views expressed in individual volumes, however, are not necessarily those of the publishers.

VOLUMES IN THE SERIES

1 *European Communities*,
  John Paxton
2 *Arab Regional Organizations*,
  Frank A. Clements
3 *Comecon: The Rise and Fall of an
  International Socialist
  Organization*, Jenny Brine
4 *International Monetary Fund*,
  Anne C. M. Salda
5 *The Commonwealth*, Patricia M.
  Larby and Harry Hannam
6 *The French Secret Services*, Martyn
  Cornick and Peter Morris

7 *Organization of African Unity*,
  Gordon Harris
8 *North Atlantic Treaty Organization*,
  Phil Williams
9 *World Bank*, Anne C. M. Salda
10 *United Nations System*, Joseph P.
  Baratta
11 *Organisation of American States*,
  David Sheinin
12 *British Secret Services*, Philip H. J.
  Davies
13 *Israeli Secret Services*, Frank A.
  Clements